LIFE
without
WALLS

*For God so loved the world that he gave his only
begotten son that whosoever believeth in him should
not perish, but have everlasting life.*

—John 3:16

CYNTHIA JONES

NEWMAN SPRINGS PUBLISHING
320 Broad Street
Red Bank, NJ 07701

First originally published by Newman Springs Publishing 2023

ISBN 979-8-88763-028-1 (Paperback)
ISBN 979-8-88763-029-8 (Digital)

Printed in the United States of America

To my mother, Bertha Lee Edwards

The Lord is my shepherd; I shall not want.
He maketh me to lie down in green pastures:
he leadeth me beside the still
waters.
He restoreth my soul; he leadeth me in the
paths of righteousness for his name's
sake.
Yea, though I walk through the valley of the
shadow of death, I will fear no evil:
for thou art with me; thy rod and thy staff they comfort me.
Thou preparest a table before me in the presence of mine enemies: thou
anointest my head with oil; my cup runneth over.
Surely goodness and mercy shall follow me all the days of my life:
And I will dwell in the house of the Lord for ever.
Amen.

—Psalm 23

As a young girl growing up in a small Southern town, I felt that life was slow and easy. I can remember my mom raising chickens, raising pigs, and having a barn in the backyard with a couple of mules. There was a well on our back porch where we went to draw up water to drink. That water was so cold and good you didn't need any ice; I don't even think we had ice back then. We kept the potty under the bed, so if anyone had to pee through the night, that's what you would use. My brother, five years older than myself, and my nephew, four years younger than me—we were mischievous. I don't think there wasn't anything that we wouldn't try.

There was a tree outside our window where we slept at night. Instead of using the front door, we would crawl out the window and climb down the tree to go outside. We walked in the woods, picking berries and plums. Not once did we come upon a snake, which was strange; I think that if we had found a snake, we would have killed it because my brother was just crazy like that. He was the only boy in the family, I was told Carolyn and Joyce took Frederick up in a tree; he fell from the tree and landed on his head. I don't know what it is about Southern people from Alabama and climbing trees. My mother always said that once that happened to her son, something wasn't right; my mother felt like that fall that my brother had as a baby made him mentally challenged.

One day my brother was riding his bicycle like he was Evel Knievel. He was riding back and forth up and down the road, back and forth up and down the road. My mother kept telling my brother to stop riding that bike like that. Of course, he didn't listen. Next thing we knew, he went airborne and landed the bicycle on the front porch of the house. We thought the fool had killed himself, but he didn't. You know parents didn't take their kids to the doctor back then. They would always do home remedies. My mom told him, "Did I not tell you to sit your ass down somewhere?"

Boy, it was funny to me, but I knew he was in pain; at the same time, it wasn't funny. We watched him walk around the house for weeks at a time, holding those ribs. I felt sorry for him, but that didn't stop him because he was just like the Energizer Bunny, ready to get at it again. Later somebody gave him a black pony that he named Midnight. My brother would ride the pony like he was driving a car. He didn't have a saddle, just a bridle in the pony's mouth, and I mean he would ride that sucker. I'm telling you my brother is just as unpredictable today as he was back then; it's a damn shame. He will always be on full speed ahead.

One day my mother was washing clothes on the back porch. We had the washing machine that had the part at the top that wrings the clothes out. It had to be done by hand. We weren't supposed to play with the washing machine. Being the daredevils that we were, hey, we were going to play with that washing machine anyway. First, we were just watching the clothes go round and round, and my nephew decided to start placing the clothes in the top loader. While we were placing the clothes in the top loader, my nephew's arm got stuck in the loader. We couldn't get his arm out; he was screaming. We didn't know what to do. We were scared, so we ran because we thought his arm was broken. My mother and sister heard all the commotion. They ran to the back porch. They saw that his arm had gotten stuck in the top loader, and they were hollering themselves, and they eventually got his arm unstuck, but they blamed my brother and myself because we were the oldest, and we got a whipping; my nephew didn't.

Like I said, that didn't stop us from being adventurous. We did it all. We would watch my brother shoot my mother chickens in the head with his BB gun. We would watch him choke her chickens until they died, and we would go to the henhouse and break eggs and whip the pigs. We would play outside from sunup until sunset, making mud pies and catching lightning bugs in a jar and watching them light up at night—it was so exciting. My mother smoked cigarettes back then; they were called Prince Albert tobacco that she had to roll up in Top paper. We would sneak in her room where she had a wooden heater to keep her room warm in the wintertime, and we would pick the butts out of the heater and go outside and smoke them. When we couldn't get the butts from the heater, we would go out in the woods and get what they call rabbit sticks, and we would smoke them. Hey, we had to create our own fun. We didn't have many toys to play with, so make-believe was the name of the game.

We had a cow that I had gotten attached to. I named her Betsy. I would go and talk to Betsy every day.

My mom noticed that I had gotten attached to Betsy. She told me one day, "Don't get too attached to that cow 'cause I'm taking her to the slaughterhouse, and she will be on the table soon."

I cried out, "No, Momma, don't take her there. They will kill her."

She said, "I know."

I cried. I knew my mom was taunting me. One day, I went to play with Betsy, and I couldn't find her. I ran in the house, and I asked my mom, "Where is Betsy?"

She replied, "In the freezer."

I burst out crying. I said, "Why you do that? She was my friend," and my mom said, "And now she is our dinner."

I started crying again, and I vowed that I would not eat her, and my mom said, "You will never know the difference."

I cried again, and everyone was laughing at me. That was my very first pet that died, and I don't remember eating her, but they would remind me at dinnertime, "You know you are eating Betsy." That was cruel, and now it's funny, but my feelings were truly hurt.

After Betsy, I always had a pet, but it would be a pet that no one wanted to eat.

My mother had a sister that lived down the road from us. We enjoyed going to her house all the time because she had so many children and grandchildren. It was lots of people to play with, and quite a few were in our age group. But one of my aunts' daughters had a son. He was her only child. He was the apple of her eyes. He didn't do anything wrong. He was the best dressed to me. He had the biggest head, the biggest eyes, and the deepest dimples I had ever seen. He was a cute little feller, but she didn't think he did anything wrong.

She would always say, "Don't anyone mess with Charles."

When I leave here, it was always "Don't mess with Charles." While I am gone, it was like she had an English accent when it came to his name because he was the greatest kid ever. Of course, we knew better. He knew that his mother was going to take up for him regardless of what he did. We were afraid of him because we knew when the grown-ups left, we were in trouble. He would go to the kitchen, get the biggest knife he could find, and run us with that knife practically all day long.

While the older kids walked in the woods and smoked weed all day and drank beer, they thought we didn't know it, but we did; but through it all, we still had fun. At the end of the day, we would play hopscotch, and we would use broken Coke bottles for tokens to go to the next base so you could jump. We would take old beer cans and smash into the heel of our shoes, and we were clacking around all day—I mean we just made up stuff. It was just hilarious, now that I think about it, but fun at the same time.

My mother was a hardworking woman. She raised seven kids by herself, and I'm the baby. She cleaned White people's houses. We love Ms. Pearson. We would go up to her house, and she would give us cakes, fruits, and candy. She was a nice old White lady. After Ms. Pearson passed away, my mom got a job at the local plant where they made lady bras. I can remember back to the age of four or five, my mother would leave me with my father while she worked. He would always tell me not to tell my mother where we had been throughout the day, and guess what, she would always ask me, "What y'all do today? Where y'all go today?"

I would always hear in my mind from my father, "Don't tell your mother anything," so that's what I did; I would say, "We didn't go anywhere, Mother," teaching me at a young age how to lie. I came to realize that that was so horrible. By me being young, I didn't realize how many women my father was dating behind my mother's back while she was at work. I didn't know he had made a pass at my second-oldest sister until I heard my mother and my sister arguing about him. My sister did not want him back in the house; she was afraid, and to make matters worse, my mother always made sure that the best part of the chicken was left for my father at dinnertime, and he didn't even have a job.

After my father found out that my sister told my mother that he made a pass at her, he got all of my sister's clothes and took them outside and set them afire. Oh, my sister was furious. My sister was angrier than Cooter Brown on a hot summer day.

My sister told me, "That man is not your father, and don't call him that again."

I was a child. I was confused. I didn't know what to say or do, but I stopped calling him "father," and I just started calling him by his name because I didn't know what to do, and back then, you did what grown-ups told you to do. My father did move out of the house. He didn't stay with us anymore. My mother continued to date him. He came over very often. She was in love with this man, and she put up with all his cheating and all the craziness that he took her through.

When my sisters would be in the living room with their boy-friends or their dates, I would always peep around the corner and watch them kiss; so one night, I was watching one of my sisters and her boyfriend. They were having an argument, and after a while, he slapped her, and what did he do that for? My mother came from that back room after she heard my sister hollering, and she told that guy if he didn't get away from there, she knew something. Boy, he got gone, and I don't remember seeing him again, but I do remember that I had another sister who was going to marry this guy, and he was from up north, and my mother didn't trust him, so he had asked my sister to marry him.

My mother said, "You're not marrying that man."

My sister said, "Yes, I am, and you can't stop me."

They got into a tussle in the kitchen, and my mother beat my sister up in the kitchen and took that ring and threw it out the door and told her, "You're not marrying that man," and she didn't marry that man because my mother was the queen of her castle, and you did as she said.

My mother had to help raise her younger siblings after her mother died. There were five of them, and my mother was the oldest. My mother told us that she had a daughter at thirteen years old and that her mother wouldn't let her tell anyone that she had a baby. Her mother told everyone that this was her child. My mom treated her daughter like she was her younger sister. When my mother's mother passed away, my mom had to step into the role of her mother cooking, cleaning and working whilst her father taught her how to make moonshine and wine. My mom's father met a woman that he married and had four boys with her, and he also had a daughter by another woman, and they lived in Florida. I was told once my oldest sister became of age, my mom told her that she wasn't her sister, that she really was her mother but that her mom lied to keep people from knowing the truth, so I understood why my mom was so tough, brave, and strong.

My mom bootlegged on the side; she sold moonshine and muscadine wine. I remember we all had to run in the woods, and we hid one night because the police found out she was bootlegging, and she hid all the moonshine in the woods. The police didn't find us. My mom was smart. We stayed in the woods until the coast was clear. My mother was a tall, slim, dark-skinned woman with beautiful long black hair, and she was very attractive. My father always accused her of dating the men that stopped by and purchased moonshine from her. He was jealous because he knew what he was doing, so he thought my mother was doing the same thing; but honestly, she was just selling moonshine, making money on the side.

My mother said that there was this one guy that you know would have too much to drink, and he would make passes at her; my father didn't like that. This one time this guy stopped by, and he made a pass at my mom. My dad reached in his pocket, got his pocketknife, and sliced this man's throat. My mom said she thought that man was going to bleed to death in her house. She was so afraid; she was just devastated. Upon numerous arguments with my father, one night he told my mother to take him up the road to someone's house, so she gathered me up, got some of my cloth diapers, and we all got in the car, and my mother was driving. My father asked my mother to stop on the side of the road so that he could take a pee, so my mother pulled beside the road, and he got out the car, and she said the whole time she kept her eyes in the rearview mirror so that she could see what he was doing because she just knew in her spirit something wasn't right.

He walked to my mother's side of the car, on the driver's side, and he asked her to get out, and she said, "Why? What do you want?"

He said, "Get out of the car, Bertha. I'm sick of your shit. Get out of the car."

She said, "Travis, I'm not getting out of this car. This baby is in this car. I'm not getting out of this car. What do you want? You can wait until we get home."

He said, "Now get out of the car 'cause I'm going to kill your motherfucking ass. Get out of the car."

My mother couldn't talk any sense into him. She always carried her pistol in my diapers when she traveled at night, plus her mind told her to make sure to take her pistol this time. She left me in the car. She grabbed my cloth diapers with the pistol wrapped inside them, and she got out the car, and she said that he was kind of drunk, so he started to push on her, and she said she kept telling him, "Travis, leave me alone. I don't want to do this with you tonight. Leave me alone. I don't want to fuss. I don't want to argue—just leave me alone. Get back in the car so we can go back to the house."

He said, "No, bitch, I'm going to kill you tonight."

She said when he lunged at her, she unwrapped those cloth diapers, and she pulled her gun out, and she said she aimed it at him, and she told him, "If you take another step, I'll blow your head off," and he said, "Oh, Bertha, you ain't going to shoot me. You ain't going to shoot me with that gun."

She said, "Don't make another step."

He lunged at her again. My mother shot him in the leg not to kill him but to wound him to stop him from hurting her, and he carried that bullet in his leg for the rest of his life; they remained friends until the end. My sister Annie is the second oldest of my siblings. My oldest sister, Kathleen, lived in Florida with her husband. It was just the six of us siblings living in the house with my mom. I think my mom gave my sister too much control when it came to helping with her children, and I think she did that because she was helping her pay the bills in the house, and they were having a new home built which was in both their names, giving her that enormous responsibility of helping raise her younger siblings. She felt privileged, privileged enough to help control our lives. The new house had been built, and it was just about ten miles down the road, passes the new county line in which we moved to.

My sister Carolyn had a child at the age of fifteen, while my sister Joyce had a child at the age of sixteen, and at seventeen, she became pregnant again. My sister Annie wasn't having all of them moving into the new house with all them babies. To me, this was cruel and unfortunate that Joyce wasn't going to be able to move into this nice, beautiful house that they had built. They argued about Joyce not moving into the new house. Joyce felt like an outcast, but she decided to take her two kids and move thirty minutes away to a town called Opelika, Alabama.

I just listened to everything and watched everybody so I would know how to handle the turn of events that are coming in my life. Then it was my turn to grow up and deal with my mom and my sister. As all these events began to shape my life, my mother kept us in church. I began to have love for a higher power, and I was baptized at our local church at an early age. August meeting was what we called revival. This lasted a whole week, and it was the biggest Christian day in our community. People who had moved away from Alabama would come home just for the revival, and people who didn't come to church would come just for that day, the revival. You would get a chance to meet family members that you hadn't seen in years and people of all the surrounding towns. It was a big event with lots of singing. I had gotten so excited with the Holy Ghost one night at church because this meeting lasted a whole week every year. I was singing and dancing in church, but to me, it was a holy dance.

When we got home, my mom told me, "This is not how you act in church, and I don't want you to ever behave like that again."

It really messed up my spirituality. I didn't know what to think anymore. I was supposed to love God and don't care who knows it, yet you are telling me to suppress my feelings and outburst for the Holy Ghost or God. I was confused on how I was supposed to worship. I think that started to shape a wall in my life that would eventually bring about events that would set up destruction and devastation in my life. Should I believe in God or not?

I remember when I first started going to clubs at the age of fourteen not because my mother didn't care or because she wanted me to go because I begged her to let me go. My sister said she would look after me. I enjoyed myself so much I became addicted to the club life. I started going out from that day forward. The first club I ever went to was called The Brave New World. I couldn't stop going. Then as I got older, sixteen and seventeen years old, I would go out with my girlfriends. I was on a curfew, but that didn't mean anything to me at that time. I live to go out to any club on the weekend. It didn't matter, and when I say we went out every weekend, we did just that.

I would dance all night. I love to dance, but when it was time for me to go to church, I had lost that drive and the spirit. I would tell my nephew to go inside the church, but I would sit in the car and go to sleep because I had stayed out all night, and I didn't want to go to sleep in church because I knew that someone would tell my mom, and I would get in trouble, not knowing that the spy was in the car with me—my own nephew. So my mom knew anyway; she just wanted me to tell her the truth. She was trying to see if I was going to lie about not going into the house of worship. When she asked me how the service was and I would say it was good and she would ask what the preacher talked about, I couldn't answer her, so that led to a whipping. I didn't stop going to the clubs and I continued to go to Bible study and falling asleep doing class.

I was a pretty good dancer, but I couldn't keep that doggone curfew for nothing in the world. My mom would ask me why I was late coming home, and I would always lie to her because I was having fun. I would hide from her at the basketball games at my school just to hang out with my friends. I stayed in trouble with my mom about going out and staying past my curfew, so she always waited up for me to come home, and sometimes she would beat me and sometimes she wouldn't, but this particular night, she decided that she was going to beat the shit out of me for not keeping her curfew. I didn't even care about the beatings anymore because whether I came home early or late, I was going to get a whipping. My mom didn't believe in talking things out to resolve our issues; she believed in violence. I truly believe this is how she was raised. She got so mad at me. She insisted on beating me that night. I ran to her car and locked the doors. This woman was so mad that she went in the house, came out to the car, pointed a handgun at my head, and told me if I didn't get out of the car, she was going to blow my head off.

Talk about scared—I had never been so scared in my life, and being sixteen years old didn't help. When that didn't work—her pulling the gun out on me trying to get me out the car—she went back in the house. I got out the car, and I ran for my life. I went to a neighbor's house, and I got him to take me to my favorite aunt's house where I hid for three days. They knew I was there; I didn't have anywhere else to go, plus this was my favorite Aunt Mavis, so my mom sent my sister, the big bad wolf, to get me because my aunt kept telling my mother that I wasn't at her house and she didn't know where I was.

My aunt had left and went to work, and I was with my older cousin. There was a knock at the door. It was my sister. My cousin was talking to her, and my sister just forced herself in the house, and my cousin kept telling her I wasn't there, that they had not seen me, and she couldn't just walk all over their house.

My sister said, "Oh, she's in this house, and I'm going to find her."

I hid under the bed. I heard my sister and cousin fighting. My sister burst in the room, where I was hiding under the bed. She dragged me from under the bed, and she commenced to whipping my ass. My sister took me home, and they talked about me for weeks. I never left home again, but I didn't stop partying either—I couldn't.

Graduation from high school was going to be the best time of my life, to be free from whipping, from my sister ratting me out to my mother. Furthermore, free from those early-morning defamation-of-character conversations they would have in the kitchen over coffee. I know when I turn eighteen years old, there will be no more curfews, no more watching, waiting on me all night long to see what time I'm coming home. I could go to any club I want anytime I want—every weekend if I like. So you know, I like meeting different types of guys and having good conversation. You know I like this smooth, sexy type of guy that was going to break your heart. Why do we get involved with those kinds of guys, not to mention they're good in bed and they always lie to us? I'm convinced this is the reason we can't let these guys go, and I always ended up with the abusive guy. Not all were, but majority of my partners were abusive in some type of way.

I would say I was about eleven years old or twelve. I rode with my so-called father that I wasn't sure if he was my father or not, according to my family, but I enjoyed the rides anyway. We would go to the next town over which was about twenty minutes away. We would sit at the pharmacy outside on the bench, and he knew everyone, and everyone knew him. He would tell me stories about people's lives. It was interesting, and we would just sit there and laugh and talk, and he would buy me ice cream and candy.

I enjoyed spending time with my father. It reminded me of the old times when we were riding together. But on this particular drive, it felt different. I could just feel in my spirit something just wasn't right. I had this ball in the pit of my stomach that said something is wrong. My father wasn't looking right. He was not sounding right, and he kept staring at me. Why? This was not going to be good. He pulled off the road, and we're in the country. He slowly moved his hand on my thigh. That's when I knew what I thought I felt in my spirit wasn't wrong. I was scared out of my life. My father, the man I admired, was trying the unthinkable with his daughter. The closer he got to me, the closer I'd lean to the passenger door. I think he could sense my fear. He probably realized I would tell my mother. He waited for a second as if he was thinking about what he was getting ready to do, and he looked at me and then he moved back to the driver's side. He didn't say anything to me, and I didn't say anything to him, and we drove off. I never looked at him the same. I couldn't wait to get home.

I did tell my mother later. Of course, she didn't believe me, but I never rode with this man again. I believe what my sisters said. He had tried to have sex with all of them. I didn't have any more respect for him. Another wall was being torn down in my life. So at that point, I never stopped wondering, is this truly my father? Because in my mind, my father wouldn't hurt me like that because a true man and father would not do that to his child, wouldn't let himself even imagine such a terrible act.

Like most girls around thirteen or fourteen years old, I was interested in boys. So we had a family friend who I met at school. This guy liked me a lot, but I wasn't into him; I just liked him as a friend, but everyone in my family loved him. He would come to our house every day to play cards and dominos. We would have fun with him. He and my sister were the best two players. Everyone thought he was the one for me except me. He always asked me out on dates, so I was kind of in a relationship with him. My mother loved him, my brother, and all my sisters. Then he asked my mother if I could go with him on Sunday evenings to his mom's house.

At first we would just go to his mom's house, stay for a little while, and he would take me back home with no strings attached. He even taught me how to drive. He would say, "You see that yellow line with the lights? If you hit those lights, you have crossed the middle of the road to the other driver's side, so don't hit the lights."

To this day, when I drive, I can remember this guy telling me not to cross the yellow line. It's funny how that got stuck in my memory. Every time he wanted me to go with him to his mother's house, of course, my mother agreed; I was like, *Say no*, in my mind. At one point, I told her to tell him I couldn't go, and she replied, "Why not? That's a nice guy for you. I knew what his intentions are because he started to ask me, so I know what he wants," but she didn't; I just liked him like a friend.

He asked my mom if he could take me to his mom's house, but this was on a Friday night, not our Sunday date, when we passed his mom's house.

I asked him, "Where are we going?"

He said, "My brother is having a party at his house, and I didn't think your mom would let you go to a house party, so it got you out the house, right?" but when we get to his brother's house, no one was there.

I said, "I thought your brother was having a party."

He replied, "No, I just wanted to spend some time with you alone."

Oh my god, I knew what that meant. I was a virgin, and he knew that. He convinced me to go in the bedroom with him, that everything would be all right. I really didn't want to do this. I was so afraid. We lay on the bed. He started to take off his clothes. I was scared.

I said, "I don't want to get pregnant. My mom would kill me."

He said, "I won't get you pregnant, I promise. I will pull out before I let that happen."

I said, "You promise."

He replied, "Yes." Plus, he said if I didn't have sex with him, he would tell my mom that I was a slut and I've been sleeping around with guys. I was horrified because I knew that my mom didn't believe me about my dad. So I did it—the unthinkable. It was the most horrible, painful feeling I had ever had, and I didn't enjoy it at all. I hated him even more. Every day he would remind me when he comes to our house to play cards to keep my mouth shut, or my mother would know that I was a hot ass and had been having sex, which was not true.

I guess this guy was obsessed with me because he would go through my locker at school, and I didn't know it. He was doing that until one day when I was eating lunch. He came to my table and asked me about a letter that I wrote a guy from the previous school I had attended. He got so mad, and he started yelling at me and beating on the table, and the principal was called. Because he was, like, out of control, and we went to the principal's office, and he was still out of control, the principal called the police, and he was suspended from school. After that, I broke up with that nut, and I didn't want nothing else to do with him from that moment on.

These events would continue to shape walls that men that I would meet would tear down in my life. One night I went out on a date with a guy I knew from my school. We were just friends; I liked him a little. He was kind of cute, but not really my type. So he asked me out on a date, and I said, "Sure, a date, of course."

We went to the movies as he suggested, and then before he took me home, he said, "Let's go to lover's lane hang out and watch the stars."

I thought that would be cool, so I said okay, not knowing that he had other plans for me. As we sat there and got comfortable, we got out the car, laughing and joking around. We sat on the hood of his car. We did watch the stars, and it started to get late, so he did make his move.

He said, "You know. You're going to give it up voluntarily. If not, I'm going to leave you out here to walk home."

Now he just went from Mr. Nice Guy to Mr. I Don't Know Who You Are Right Now At This Point. We weren't nowhere close to my house, and I didn't want to be left out there alone, and I didn't want to have sex against my will, but at this point, I'm about to be date raped. I was scared again. Why do I keep getting myself in these predicaments? Better yet, what's wrong with these guys? What's wrong with me? So to keep from walking home, I had to figure something out. Have sex or walk home and take a chance at getting kidnapped? So I had sex with him. I see why he date-raped girls; he's got an itsy-bitsy spider, ha ha, and he took me home, and I never spoke to him again.

Just when I thought I was all finished with boys, I was walking the hallway, minding my own business, and this guy approached me. He said hello. When I looked up at him, it was the coolest guy in school—the most popular guy. My heart started racing inside. I thought I was going to melt. When he asked me out on a date, I was like asking myself, *What do you want with me?* Even though I was cute myself, I was like, *This guy wants to take me out on a date!*

Of course, I said yes. I couldn't wait for our first date. We started dating, and I was crazy about this guy. But guess what? The crazy fool approached me again one day at school and said, "I thought you told me that you would never date a guy like that because he is a playboy."

I just looked at him and said, "Oh, well," and walked away.

I found out what a guy calling himself a playboy is all about. He was dating me and everybody else. He used me up like a yo-yo—up and down, side to side, back and forth. Ah, I finally just woke up and smelled the coffee that this relationship was headed nowhere. He had a girl in every little, small town. Boy, I mean small towns. Everyone knows your business, and you eventually will run into the other woman, and this is what happened—I ran into the other girlfriend that later became his wife.

I was so upset. *Heartbroken* wasn't the word, but I had to get past it. I had to pick up the pieces and get back in the scene and start doing what I know to do best—going back to the club. I was giving up on love in relationships—there was no one out there for me—but, ladies, we must stop thinking that our high school love is going to be the only one for us. You know why? Because people change and circumstances change, and we grow interest in other people; that's why it's called puppy love, but being a teenager, it's hard to grasp a hold of that scenario. Life always teaches us lessons that you will not forget and you can pass along to your children or family.

So I thought it's time to buckle down and focus on me. By now I had finished high school. I was eighteen years old. You had three choices in my mother's house after you graduated from high school: You could either go to college, the military, or get a regular job, and I decided it would be college for me. Like I planned, I applied for college, got accepted, went to visit the school, and enrolled. I decided that I needed a car so that I could travel back and forth home whenever I decided to come home. My mother helped me get this car because she was so excited about me going to college.

Getting the car was a big mistake. I should have never gotten that car. That car kept me from going to school. That car was a means of transportation for me and my friends. It was a means of getting around to clubs and partying. It was a means for me and my cousin to switch cars—we had twin vehicles. She had a white Corolla, I had a yellow Corolla, and we thought we had it going on at that time. We would switch cars, you know, to meet guys and be in a different car so no one would know who was seeing whom—all my idea because she didn't always want to do the devilish things that I wanted to do. I always had to beg her to help me pull off some unspeakable acts. She would be mad and start fussing, but my cousin always came through for her girl. You know that was life to us—all fun and games.

So I decided that I would get a job because all my friends were working at plants at the time. I got a job in a place called Alex City. The plant was called Russell Mill. They made athletic attire. I learned a lot about setting sleeves and sewing the hem of shirts. It wasn't a bad job, though it didn't pay much at that time. I think we made $3.25 an hour.

I was very good friends with this girl named Tammy. She was my classmate as well. We worked at the mill together. We came up with the idea to get paid for being out of work. You know if someone passed in your family, you get paid for those three days. So we became cousins on the job, and we would kill off relatives, but the relatives were already dead—you know, grandmothers, grandfathers—someone we could get paid, for we felt like, hey, we weren't going to get any karma from this because these people are dead. But it was funny to us because we had to go into the office, put on this front like we're crying about our relatives, and make up some story, a sympathy speech to our supervisor and get those three days off work, get paid, and go party. That was so cruel, but we were young and stupid—you do things like that when you're young. That's part of growing up.

I was doing fine until I met another guy hanging with some of my girlfriends. Those guys from the eighties and the nineties had a swag about themselves that could make any girl lose her mind. Before meeting this guy, I heard a lot about him. He was older, more mature than the guys I dated in high school; he had a very nice black Camaro; you know, he was another one of those playboys that I seemed to now be attracted to. So when I met him and he was all of what I thought he was and a bag of chips, oh yes! When he asked me out, of course, I was ready to say yes.

We started dating, I had no idea that he had a main girlfriend. I kind of figured that he talked to other girls but he had a main girlfriend. He would come visit me at my mom's house. He would take me out. There was nothing that was telling me this man was not on the up-and-up. He treated me like I was the only one. He treated me like gold when we were together. He treated me like I was his woman when he would come to my mom's house to visit me or date night. When it gets to be 10:00 p.m. at night and he's still there—you know, my mom was raised in a time where guys were not allowed to stay past, I believe, eight or nine o'clock at night at a girl's house—but my mom let my guest stay until 10:00 p.m.

One night he was there, and he stayed past ten o'clock at night. We were sitting in the living room, talking. In came a shoe—someone threw a shoe in the living room where we were. We started laughing, like, "Who threw this shoe?"

I picked the shoe up, and I walked in the next room where my mom was and asked her, "Did you throw this shoe in the room?"

She said, "Yes, because that means it's time for him to go home."

I said, "Are you for real?"

She was like, "Yeah, it's ten o'clock. He needs to go home. It's time for you to go to bed. He needs to respect people's homes. Didn't I tell you he couldn't stay past ten o'clock?"

I went back in the room where he was, and I told him my mom said he had to leave. But that was the most hilarious thing that happened to me during my dating experience because my mom did not like this guy at all. She knew of his reputation, and she didn't trust him. She said he had a sneaky grin about himself, and she knew that he was up to no good. She wanted me to have nothing to do with him, but I was in love with him, and she could not stop that, and love had conquered all. But the relationship that he had with his main girlfriend topped everyone else, so when I asked him about the main girlfriend, he was like, "No, we're just friends."

So I didn't care at that point because what he said was what I believed! Me, of course, not knowing that he would take me out on a date and then he would take her out on a date; but of course, she was, like I said, the main girlfriend. When I saw them at the club together, I was so mad because he had lied to me, and I went up to him in front of her and confronted him: "You need to tell me something?" Telling me one thing and I'm seeing something else, and all my girlfriends saying, "She is the main girlfriend. You just need to leave him alone. That guy is not good for you."

I still wasn't convinced when someone is telling you sweet things and ensuring you that they care about you and taking you out and doesn't care who saw you together. I mean, I believe what he said, but he was showing me something different, and he only took me to his mom's house one time; and while I was there, his mom told me about the main girlfriend.

I was thinking to myself about his mom, *Why are you telling me this? You should stay in a mom's place. This isn't something you should be talking to a young girl about, another woman that your son is dating.* I didn't respect her for that, not at all because you shouldn't be talking to me about this. I believe she told me because she didn't like me; she liked the other girl. So me and the main girlfriend, we would often have run-ins about this guy. We would argue about going with him—who was his girlfriend?—and most of the time I would be the one who started the argument because I was in love, and I guess she had already been in love for a long time, and she was unbothered because she knew she had her fingers wrapped around him.

They never married until this day, and I don't even know to this day if he even ever told her we lost a child together, and that really hurt both of us, and I regret to God to this very day that I lost my child. I mourn for my child. I wish I could have seen my child grow up and experience all the things that you would experience with your first child, my firstborn, but we were not given that privilege, not having the opportunity to parent our child together, because this child was made from love, and he expressed how he regretted it as well. So that bond that we built with that child will never die even though the future has come time and time again, and we were not in it together, but we will forever have a child together, and this is what you call love—to this day.

But the years of abuse that I was about to suffer during these marriages is unimaginable. In the men that I chose to marry, family are also road blockers in this life we live. Before this first marriage, living with my family even though we sometimes argued and fought, we were a close family. We were all that we had. We didn't have fathers that raised us, only our mother, but my mother wasn't an affectionate person. She didn't show you love. I don't think that she was raised where she was shown love. I think she was raised hard and went through hard times, and her being oldest of her siblings, she had to grow up fast because her mother died young and she had to step in and raise the rest of her siblings, which made her strong and firm, and she expected you to be the same way, but sometimes some of us need a little more affection. Some of us need a little bit more love. Some need to be nurtured. I don't think she knew how to do that.

This was where my sister Carolyn stepped in. She was like a mother to me. She would take me and her son out to the movies. She would take us out of town with her when she lived in North Carolina. She showed us how life really was, and we got to a chance see how beautiful outside of Alabama really was. We were friends before sisters. You could go to her and talk to her about anything. You could tell her your deepest, darkest secrets, and she would always have an answer for you, or she could help you figure out what was going on in your life. I could talk to her about my boyfriends, and once I got married, I could talk to her about my marital problems as well.

I had another sister, Joyce. She was my best friend also, but I couldn't talk to her like I could talk to Carolyn because Joyce was like my mom—she was tough. She didn't take any wooden nickels. I mean, if you stepped on her toe, she might punch you in the face. She had a temper like my mom. Carolyn, she was more understanding and willing to talk about any situation. If talking didn't solve the problem, this was when she would be ready to fight. We were happy, and we didn't really realize we were poor because we lived a good life.

My sister Carolyn lost both of her breasts before the age of thirty, and if you knew her, you wouldn't think that this life-changing situation affected her in any way. She chose the reconstructive surgery after her mastectomy, and I never saw her cry or have pity for herself. She was an example of strength that I had never seen before in my life. She was my hero, and I never got a chance to tell her how much I admired her. If someone would have told me that we both would become successful entrepreneurs and that those businesses would bring animosity into our relationship, I would have said never.

Never say never because you just never know. Envy, jealousy, competition, bickering, arguments, and control can tear families apart. But what I did not realize at the time was that as we grew older and as our lives changed, our decisions in our lives changed, and our family would fall apart. After her implant surgeries and she started to have problems with her breast—the silicone was leaking throughout her body—she entered a class action lawsuit where she was waiting on millions of dollars.

Money can change a person because she promised us the world; she said we would never have anything to worry about again, that she would make sure we lived a comfortable life, and we believed her. We waited just like she did. It took a while, but eventually she received it. And I do acknowledge that it was her money and not our money. Don't make promises that you don't intend on keeping, but we didn't let the money stop our relationship at that time because she would buy you mostly anything you asked for within reason. We didn't have a perfect family relationship as this story continues. You will find out that the devil was in the details all along—family, marriages, everything was just a façade—but it was funny how the laugh was always on me.

No family is perfect no matter what kind of picture they paint for the outside world. One of the main reasons I was ready to move away from home was because I wanted out of our dysfunctional family. I watched my sisters encounter unhealthy interactions with my mother and second-oldest sister. I was always headstrong, stubborn, hardheaded, determined, and was an already-had-my-mind-made-up type of person—traits of being a Taurus—but my mother called it "acting like your father."

My cousin and her boyfriend didn't know they were getting ready to introduce me to another wall of destruction in my life. So marriage number one. I wasn't dating anyone. I had just lost my first child. I wasn't with the father of my child. Is there anyone out in this world for me? If I have to say so myself, I was a nice-looking girl. I had long hair. I was bowlegged. I was easy on the eyes. So it wasn't that I couldn't get a boyfriend; it was the men that I chose to have in my life weren't for me.

I met my first husband through my cousin; she and I would always hang out together. She was dating a guy from Georgia, and I believe she had fallen in love with this guy. You could tell it in her voice when she spoke of him—she was head over heels. He had served in the Army, so he knew his way around, and they had good times together. They thought about me: "How convenient, little old Cynthia isn't dating anyone. Let's introduce her to a friend of mine." They asked me if I wanted to go double-dating with them to meet his friend. I said, "Sure. No problem."

When I met the guy, he was a nice-looking guy, brown skin—not chocolate like I normally like—naturally curly hair, tall, and slim. He was okay. After that date, he would drive down from Atlanta to spend the weekend with me. He would take me to Atlanta to spend the weekend with him, and I said to myself this guy must really like me. He was driving all the way from Atlanta, Georgia, to see li'l me. I felt special because no one had ever driven that far from home to come see me. I don't remember how long we dated, but I guess he was looking for a wife, and I was looking for a way out of Alabama.

When his friend asked me, "If he asked you to marry, would you marry him?"

I said, "If he asks me, I will say yes." Here is my opportunity to get away from Alabama.

I don't know how much longer we dated before he popped the question "Will you marry me?" And I said, "Yes, I will."

We did just that. We prepared for a wedding. In a wedding, it was all his family in attendance. It was so beautiful, but the day of the wedding, everyone was crying in my family. I guess no one had left the nest and moved to another state but me. My brother was crying, my cousin was crying—and she hooked me up with the guy. Everybody was crying. I was crying. I was like, "Dude, I really got to go live with you in Atlanta, Georgia. Now I have changed my mind."

When we left Alabama headed to Georgia, I was still crying. When we got to the hotel room, I was crying. Instead of us making out and enjoying our marriage, celebrating the relationship, I was crying. My new husband was trying to calm me down. He was telling me everything was going to be all right and that I could see my family whenever I wanted; just don't cry. I eventually stopped crying, but I still didn't want him to touch me.

Sometimes you got to be careful what you wish for—your wishes just might come true. I knew I wasn't in love. Camp Hill being such a small town, I wanted a taste of the city life. I would get in his car sometime at night and just ride by myself downtown and look at the tall buildings and just enjoy the scenery. I knew he knew I was homesick, so he tried to convince me that we would be the perfect family. It was just going to be me and him against the world. I could see through all that smoke and smooth talk. It was going to be me in isolation from the world, and I didn't want that. It was like he became obsessed, overprotective.

He told me, "You don't need anybody, and I don't need anybody. We got each other." I needed family, friends, and conversation from other people. Only surrounding myself with him wasn't going to work out for me.

I would take him to work often on some days, and when I felt homesick, I would sneak home to Alabama to visit my family. I always arrived back in Georgia in time to pick him up from his job. I was pretty sure he didn't know of my back-and-forth trips unless he had been checking the mileage on the car, which I wouldn't put past him.

Carolyn came to visit us.

Husband replied, "Is she staying a couple of days?"

I said, "Yes."

I could tell he was getting frustrated, that he really didn't want her there. He pulled me to the side and asked me how long she was going to be staying with us. I told him that she would be leaving soon. One evening, we were waiting for him to come home from work so he could eat with us. We all were sitting at the kitchen table, and as we were eating, this man was looking and acting crazy. I had a feeling that he was going to say something to her, but I was hoping that he wouldn't. He put his fork down on the table, and he looked at my sister, and he swallowed his food, and he said, "If you are not bringing anything into this house, you can't eat at this table. You got to bring something in," meaning no job to pay for food—you're not welcome to eat here. I could have slapped his ass myself. I felt so embarrassed and ashamed. Is this the kind of fool I married? My mom taught me that you can always feed a person if you can't do anything else.

She said, "I will leave if I'm not wanted here," and he said, "Yes, I want you to leave."

I couldn't believe he did that, and I said to my sister, "Don't listen to him. You can stay here if you like."

She said, "No. He asked me to leave, and I'm going to leave—but he didn't have to do me like that. He waited until we were eating to put me out. He could've done this after we ate."

Either way, it was a messed-up situation. Zack didn't consider either one of our feelings. We are sisters, and that meant a lot to us at that time. We were used to looking out for each other. I could see the hurt in my sister's eyes, and there was nothing I could do. Watching her leave that day hurt my heart. I think he realized that he was wrong regarding the way he treated her because he tried to console me after she left, explaining why he had to put his foot down in his house. After this event, his actions would prove to be calculated. Even the girls that I became friends with on my jobs were greeted with a nasty attitude. It was like he didn't want them to visit me. Deloris was one of my friends, and we would visit each other often. One day she said Cynthia, "What's wrong with your husband? I don't think he wants me to come around to visit."

I said, "Girl, this man wants me to live in this world with only him in my life. He doesn't want me to have family nor friends."

"Girl, ignore him 'cause that's what I do."

And we laughed.

When I would go out with my lady friends, he would get so upset with me, but I didn't care. I was miserable. I think he noticed that I was becoming increasingly unhappy with this relationship. So to cheer me up, he decided to take me to Disney World. We tried to ride all the rides because the last time that I had been to Disney

World was when my sister Carolyn took us; I think I was about maybe fourteen or fifteen years old.

After getting back home from Florida maybe two to three weeks later, I started feeling sick, so I went to the doctor, and the doctor confirmed that I was indeed pregnant. One night we were sitting on the bed, watching TV. I started feeling something warm between my legs and I looked down, and it was blood everywhere. I started screaming, and I started feeling pressure, and I told him to call my doctor, and he did.

The doctor stayed on the phone with me and asked has anything passed from me, and I was like, "No, but it feels like something is trying to pass."

He said, "Go in the bathroom and catch whatever comes out of you in a cup."

So that's what I did. I went to the bathroom and popped out this little white pig-shaped thing inside the cup. I took it to the emergency room with us. After the examination, the doctor said, "You have had a miscarriage, and we're going to have to do a D and C on you." I was so heartbroken.

I had a name for this child—a girl's name. I wrote that name down, and I put it in my wallet because I didn't ever want to lose that name. In case I ever had a girl, I would already have her name. I had that name in my wallet for five years before I would become a mother of a little girl.

But living with my husband, I had a couple of jobs here and there downtown where I rode a MARTA bus to the train station to get to work downtown and coming back home. This was just too much. I was miserable. He bought me my first purebred dog, a Pekingese. I loved that dog; he was my friend. I kept getting sick and having to go back and forth to the doctor—women problems! I didn't know what was going on; I just stayed sick a lot and had a lot of trouble out of my stomach. I had an examination done with my doctor, and you know when they take you back in a little room and talk to you in private.

He was like, "I don't know how to tell you this, but your husband is too big for you."

"What do you mean too big for me?"

"I mean that's why you were having all these yeast infections and problems with your stomach—is because he's too large for you."

I said, "Oh, okay. Thank you so much, Doctor. I will let my husband know, and you have a great day."

I left the doctor's office, saying to myself, "This dude is like a mule," but for a doctor to say that blew my mind. "Hey, he's not going to keep tearing my body down."

So what am I going to do about that? I had never encountered a guy this "blessed" by God. I just wasn't the woman that could handle that blessing. My husband and I discussed the doctor's visit. We concluded nothing from that conversation, and we went on with our lives, and he continued to try to do things to make me happy so that I wouldn't leave him.

My nephew had graduated from high school. He decided to go into the Navy, so his training was out in California. The entire family was so excited about his graduation that they asked all of us to go to his naval graduation, so when I asked my husband, "Could I go with my family to California for my nephew's graduation from the Navy?" he said, "No, you can't go."

I'm not missing this trip to California, and I have never been to California in my life.

I said, "I'm going anyway," and that's what I did. I packed my bags. I waited for my family to come through Atlanta and pick me up, and I rode with them to California, and I was glad that I decided to go on that trip. I got a chance to see my nephew graduate from the Navy and then we visited some of my mother's family while we were there, and it also gave me a chance to realize that I'm not going to continue to stay with this man because I'm not in love with him. So we drove all the way back home from California, and they dropped me off in Atlanta.

This guy looked at me and spoke, "You know? You're my wife, and I asked you not to go, and you went anyway, so I feel like you need to pack your bags and go on with your family because I see now that's who you want to be with. There's no need for you to continue to be with me because you want to be with your family."

I said, I just went on a trip with my family to see my nephew graduate. What's wrong with that? A couple of days later in a heated argument he slapped me. I got on the phone and called my mother, I told her what had happened. I decided to leave Zack and return home. I packed all my clothes. I sat on the outside of the apartment with my dog, and I waited for my family to get there; and when they got there, I got in the car, went back home to Alabama. After being in Alabama a couple of weeks, then it led to a month. He would call me and ask me if I am coming home, and I would say, "No, I'm not coming back."

I guess about three weeks to a month after that, I got a letter in the mail from an attorney. They were divorce papers. I signed the papers, and I have never seen him again—that was the end of that, marrying just to move out of town and getting away from family. After the divorce, I was staying back at my mother's house. A lot of times I would hang out at my sister's apartment because she lived in town and my mother lived outside town. It was more convenient for me to stay with my sister so I could get a chance to hang out in the streets.

One afternoon, a classmate and myself decided to go out for a midnight stroll. While we were walking, just talking and laughing, this guy walked past us. He had on a pair of cycling shorts and a muscle shirt, and he had Jheri curls—all the guys had their hair like that back then. He was fine.

I said, "Who is that?"

She said, "Do you want to meet him? I know him. I can introduce you to him."

I said, "Yes, I wouldn't mind meeting him."

She called his name. He stopped, and he came back where we were, and she introduced us, and we talked for a couple of minutes, and he asked me, "How often do you hang out here at this apartment complex?"

I told him, "My sister lives out here. I be out here a lot."

So he said, "Next time I see you at your sister's house, I'll holler at you."

I said, "Okay, cool."

I started staying at my sister's apartment just so that I could see this guy, and he would come by to visit me at Morningside apartment just about every day. As the visits progressed, the vibe between us was good. I enjoyed his company. He was fun to be around, and he was very witty. He seemed like the perfect gentleman. Everything seemed like it was perfect.

Remember, there is no such thing as perfect people. They let you see what they want you to see, and they let you believe what you want to believe. It is up to you to see the bigger picture, and sometimes we miss that picture, which alters walls within our lives that puts us on a path that leads to destruction. We were falling for one another. I knew he didn't have a lot, but that didn't matter. I knew that he was a hard worker. He just needed someone to help guide him in the right direction. So one Saturday afternoon, we had a cookout at my sister's apartment, and this was the first time my family got a chance to be around him on a more personal level.

I found out something that I did not know until the cookout—this guy is a heavy drinker. At that time, I could only handle Pink Champale—that was the popular drink for a young lady back then. We did have some beers in the cooler because my brother would drink beers, and we all smoked marijuana, but Ant didn't smoke; he hated any kind of smoke. I learned he made up for that in his drinking. I noticed that he would drink beer after beer. Baby, it wasn't no shame in his game; this guy drank all the beer just about by himself.

After Ant left, my brother said, "Where you find this clown at?" My brother was so pissed off. "I purchase all this beer, and he drank it all by himself. Don't invite that motherfucker up here to nothing else we have."

It was funny at the time, but I could feel where my brother was coming from because I was shocked. We had never encountered that type of situation before; we are used to people drinking in moderation and thinking about maybe someone else would like to have a beer. That should have been a warning sign to me there's something not right about this guy, and as the saying goes "something in the milk isn't clean." I should've realized that he had a drinking problem. One thing about meeting people—you never know who they really are. You never really know a person until you live with them. That's a true statement. Whoever came up with that statement hit the nail on the head.

As we continued to date, we would go to the mall. I would pick out his clothes, his shoes. This was my opportunity to make my man the person I wanted him to be. He had the look and smelled good, and baby, he had the pizzazz. Of course, the ladies admired him. I wasn't bothered because we were together, a couple. News alert: Don't get too comfortable in your position; there is always someone waiting to replace you. Being naive at the time, this is what I wanted—no half-stepping. We complemented each other.

The drinking, the parties, always having a good time—I got caught up in all of that. Like I said, I wasn't a big drinker. Sometimes with the company that you keep, you can find yourself falling into a pattern of living just to fit right into a situation that you had no business being in the first place. So now he's my man, he's my friend, and he's my ride-or-die because I was that girl, that ride-or-die chick. I was his partner in everything that he did. Not that he was doing criminal acts, no, but just hanging out.

Being with the boys, you can sometimes get in trouble, and I hung with the boys. I enjoyed hanging out with the guys because he was a different kind of guy. I have never been around someone that didn't mind getting in trouble. Getting into fights didn't matter; I enjoyed the excitement of it all, the thrill. I felt engaged because they didn't leave me out. I had even increased in drinking. Now I'm drinking beer; I was like one of the guys. I had me a bad boy, and I was in too deep. One evening, there was a party in the complex. I was at my sister's apartment; I decided to go and check out the scenery.

I went outside. I wasn't interested in going to the party. A guy walked up to me and said, "Is Ant your dude?"

I said yes.

"Well, he is at that party kissing all over this girl named so-and-so."

I said, "Not my boyfriend," 'cause that girl got a reputation of being a garden tool—you know the rest.

So I entered the house. He was talking to her. He was all in her face. I went up to him, her, and I asked, "What's going on?" because they were just a little bit too close for me. I hit her. She started screaming and crying, but what he did to me was so embarrassing. He slapped me and had the audacity to spit in my face.

He said, "Don't you ever come looking for me again."

I left the party embarrassed, humiliated, and in pure disgust. My boyfriend had just embarrassed me in front of the whole community. I knew my family was going to find out, plus the girl pressed charges against me.

When my mother asked me if he hit me and spit in my face, I lied to her, said no, not knowing this would become the way of life for me. Rule number 1: Don't burst in a party and confront your man about another woman. I learned that he couldn't handle the truth. Red flags were all in my face, but I refused to accept the reality that this man had no respect for me as a girlfriend or person. So why I continued to plan a wedding with this man is beyond my comprehension. Another wall was placed in my life. Warnings always come before destruction. So naturally, a girl wants her father to meet her future husband.

I mentioned to Ant, "Let's go to my dad's house. He told me he would give me two hundred dollars to help me purchase this car, and I want him to meet you."

I was all excited about going to see my dad. When we arrived at his house, we got out and walked up to the door. He had the door open as usual in the summertime with the screen door locked. I knocked on the door, and he invited us in. I still could not call this man Daddy to his face; I always said "Travis." Since I had company with me, I guess he wasn't expecting me to ask for the money. Anyway we chatted for a little while, and I said, "Hey, we are going to get ready to go. I just wanted you to meet my friend. Oh, by the way, I came to pick up that two hundred dollars you told me to come and get."

When I said that, he put this stank look on his face. You know it's a level of respect for a person that anyone should have for another human being especially if you have been acknowledging the fact that this is your child. This man looked at me and didn't care that I had a friend with me. This was something that he had been wanting to get off his chest, and I just happened to open the door for him to walk all over my feelings, but this man said, "I don't have two hundred dollars to give you."

I said, "Okay, but you told me to come pick the money up. I'm just doing what you said."

When he said that my Aunt Lola told him that she didn't believe that he was my father. Why would you believe my mother's sister? First, he was relying on a statement from a sister of the lady that he was in a relationship with. Why would you say that? He believed what my Aunt said, and he told me that he didn't believe that I was his biological daughter. I wanted to burst into tears, thinking that the rumors were true, but I stood tall and remained strong. I said, "Dammit, I wasn't there, so I don't know if you planted my seed or not, but you won't have to worry about me ever again. I promise you that. I tell you I was so embarrassed and hurt, and you disrespected me in front of my friend."

I cried when we got in the car. Ant said, "He is wrong for that. He could have spoken to you about that some other time since that's the way he feels."

I couldn't wait to go home and tell my mother what he said. When I arrived at my mom's house and I told her what he said, her response was, "I bet he want tell me that he isn't your father."

I don't even know if they had DNA kits, but I wanted the truth. I never went back to that man's house, neither did I speak to him again. I wouldn't see him again until my mother begged me to go to the nursing home to see him once his condition never improved. My mom was like, "You better go see him before he passes away."

He was sent to the veterans hospital in Alexander City. I went to visit him at least four times. I told my mom, "I'm going to purchase a DNA kit, and we are going to prove once and for all if he is my father."

My mother said with confidence, "Okay, get the test."

I explained to her that all three of us will be swabbed that day, and she agreed. I went and purchased the DNA test, picked my mom up from home, and we drove to the veterans home in Alex City.

When we got to his room, I said, "Momma, I'm going to swab you first."

She said, "Okay." She opened her mouth up wide, and I swabbed her willingly, then I swabbed my dad and sealed them individually according to the direction, and then I swabbed myself. Now I have all three samples, and no one was forced to participate. So this test was performed two months before my dad passed away. While I was waiting on the results, one thing that was told to me—"What you don't know won't hurt, but the truth can sometimes kill you"—I wasn't hearing any of that. This man told me, "I am not your father," and my mom keep telling me that he is.

This is my life. I am the child born from this act, and I want to know the truth. When I received the results in the mail, I was happy. I said, "Now I got something to fight with when I go to the funeral. I'm going to show the results to my father's daughter. Lord, have mercy."

I opened the letter, and I started to read the results. The results were like this:

> Bertha Edwards Morgan is 99 percent your mother and Travis Hicks is 99.9 percent not your father.

I could have shit a brick out.

Hold up, wait a minute—this can't be right. No way is this correct.

I immediately got on the phone with a very well-known DNA company, and I explained the situation, and the tech looked up the results, and he explained to me, "Ma'am, we didn't make a mistake. These are your true results. I'm sorry, but Travis Hicks is not your father."

When I got off the phone with the representative, I was broken into pieces. He wasn't lying. That's why Travis felt in his heart that

I wasn't his child; he didn't have a connection with me. I felt like a fool. I have been lied to half of my life because he didn't really treat me like a daughter. So I called the one person who was alive—my mother—and I told her what the results said. Now I'm devastated, but she, on some bullshit, her answer was, "I told you not to go messing around with that damn man 'cause he was dying—that's why the results didn't come out right."

I said, "Momma, it's 2005. This DNA test is not wrong. Momma, forensics science people dig bodies up all the time and get DNA samples for all sorts of reasons. Surely you do realize this right now. Can you please just tell me who the other man was that you slept with so I can know my real father?"

She said, laughing, "That is your real daddy."

I wanted to tell her to stop lying, but I couldn't disrespect my mom. She didn't raise me like that, plus she would still slap the shit out of you. I felt funny when I attended the funeral and put that fake face on like "yes, I'm his daughter." The family welcomed me and my kids. My name was on the obituary, and I wanted to scream out, "It's all a lie," but I managed to make it through the day. No child deserves to go through life not knowing where your bloodline originated from; it's a child's privilege and right to know this. This event would start my quest for closure for me as a person to know my real family, and my children deserve to know who our relatives are as well; it would take me thirteen years before I would know the truth about my father.

Back to this life-changing experience that would shape a course in my life for the humiliation and disrespect for the beginning of a roller coaster ride for the next twelve years, the second marriage, July 29, our wedding day, the happiest day of my life. I knew this time that I was making the right decision. I knew this time I wasn't leaving because I didn't want to help pay bills at my mom's house, and I knew it wasn't because I was just so tired of the small town that I come from. I knew this time it was real love, that the relationship was my destiny.

The colors of my wedding was peach and white, and everyone looked so beautiful. Myself and my bridesmaids were in the room at the back of the church where I would walk down the aisle from. My sister was helping me get dressed. The bridesmaids were in and out of the room. My future sister-in-law entered the room and told us that there was a girl at the wedding that her brother used to date, and I told my sister she's got to go; she's not invited, and she's not wanted here. So my sister didn't mind telling a person what was on her mind. She said, "I will get rid of her."

She walked up to them, and she asked her, "Were you invited?"

The girl and her friend said no.

"Ah, my sister said she wants you to leave her wedding. This is her day."

The girl didn't make any remarks. They just got up out of their seats, and they left, and we laughed and laughed about the whole situation. How are you going to show up to a man's wedding that you are sleeping with and you are not the bride?

I thought the joke was on her, but I was the real dummy. This marriage was going to be the worst decision of my life—the pain, heartache, physical abuse, verbal abuse, emotional abuse, the cheating, and just the overall disrespect. I was getting ready for the trip of my life, and I was about to be taught by the best teacher in the world—my husband. I did not realize I was about to lose my self-esteem, self-worth, and all the good qualities and values, morals, and respect that I had as a person.

I didn't allow my first husband to disrespect me in any way, but I was in love this time. Cupid had me all messed up. Love is a powerful emotion that if not handled with care can destroy your life. I started to give more of me, and he gave less of him. It was like he was an emotionless creature. He made it seem so easy not to care. After the wedding, we moved in with his parents. I was cool with that because I liked his parents; they were nice people. His parents treated me nicely, and they welcomed me into their family.

I would often sit on the porch with his father and listen to all his stories of how he was the man back in the day and how he was the ladies' man. When he was getting ready to tell you a really good story, he would stand up, lick his thumb, fold it in, and slick his hair behind his ear. He also had a Jheri curl that was his signature mark—I loved it. He always bragged about how he could have married any woman he wanted other than his wife—it was funny. Every evening, when my father-in-law would get off work, he would sit on the front porch, and I would go outside and sit with him. He would send any one of us to the store to get him a six-pack of Schaefer beer every day. We would call the beer water because it was an unknown name to us. He would send you to the store with the exact change every day—nothing more, nothing less. I told my husband why he won't just buy a case because he drinks every day. My husband said he didn't want to do it like that. I was thinking this man was weird. Who does that?

His dad was hilarious. I noticed that his mom was timid and soft-spoken. I felt like she had encountered lots of abuse, but she treated me as if I was her daughter. She had only one daughter, but I was so comfortable around this lady. I watch my husband disrespect his mom, talk back to her as if she was the kid. I had never seen that before because if I would have spoken to my mom like that, she would have slapped me to the ground, so I knew I had embarked upon a different type of family.

One night, my husband and I got into an argument, and he jumped on me. I got his parents to take me home to my mother's house. At that time, we didn't have children. I should have stayed at my mother's house, but once again, I let him talk his way back into my life. After returning home to my husband at his parents' house, I don't know what occurred while I was gone, but my husband did not keep it a secret that he didn't care for his father. He always expressed to me how he didn't care for this man. Through one of our conversations, he opened up to me about what happened to them as children. He said his father had hailed them at gunpoint in their house and threatened to kill them. This was when I realized that he had also been abused, and this was why he didn't know how to treat me or anyone else. The abused sometimes becomes an abuser themselves. I said, therefore, he doesn't know how to love me.

No one has showed him love before. Sometimes you become the environment of what you came from, but you don't have to. He could have chosen a different path, but he didn't. He was going to take me down the same path that his father took his mother. We had lived with his parents for about a year. I was tired of the disrespect. I felt like we needed our own place to personalize and make it ours with own sofas, dishes, sheets, and towels, just to know that this stuff is ours and we don't have to share it with anyone.

We went out searching for an apartment in Opelika, a town which was much larger and had better job opportunities. We did move into an apartment complex. My husband eventually started to become friends with a guy downstairs. He and his friends started hanging out with my husband, and they were just like him—up to no good. My husband and the guy downstairs had become very good friends. I have to get to know people first. I just don't become friends with anybody. These people were different than the people we hung out with in the country, it took me a little longer to come around when it came to hanging out with them, but I did decide to become friends with the guy's girlfriend because we were the only two ladies among all those guys. I'm going to be honest—I didn't like the chick. I felt like she was sneaky, and I felt like she was up to something. Even though I still talked to her and we had conversations, I didn't trust her.

Then I found out I was pregnant. When a woman becomes pregnant, you know we get very emotional, and our discernment increases. When we would have gatherings with this couple or with some of their friends, I could sense that my husband had his eye on this girl and vice versa. Every time we would run into one another at a store or even at the apartment complex and Ant wasn't with me, she would always ask me, "How is Ant doing? Is he doing okay?" Not one time would she ask me how I was doing. I was the one pregnant.

I said something was fishy about this. I had gotten fed up with the staring at each other, giving each other the sexiest smiles. In my heart, I know he was sleeping with this girl, and there was nothing that was going to keep me from confronting him about it. Something was going on behind my back and her boyfriend's back, and I was going to get to the bottom of it even though I was eight months pregnant; my baby was to be born in July.

When I confronted him about the girl downstairs, he got so angry with me that Saturday morning that he jumped on me. Remember, I'm pregnant. He pushed me so hard against the dresser with the mirror that it broke, and I was still fighting back with him. When I hollered for him to stop and let me go, it seemed like he just snapped back to his self, and he saw that I was in pain. Instead of him helping me, he left. I was holding my stomach, feeling pains and so much discomfort. I just knew I was going into labor. His MO is leaving the scene of a crime. I was hurting so bad I got in the car and drove myself to the hospital, Luckily, we lived around the corner from the hospital. I called my mother, and they all came to the hospital. I told them what had happened. My mother didn't like him anyway; she said he was a coward because he beat women.

I was taken in the back, and they examined me and told me, "Yes, you're in labor."

My sister tried getting in touch with my husband, but she couldn't, so she decided to get in contact with one of his family members, and eventually, he arrived at the hospital like nothing had happened. They let him suit up. He barely made it in the room to witness his first child being born. My family was so mad because of what had happened and the fact that he almost missed the birth of his first child.

My sister asked him, "How are you going to almost miss the birth of your child, and why you put your hands on my sister?"

He didn't say anything; I guess because we were in a hospital setting.

After she was born, we moved to a small trailer on the other side of town to save some money, but then we decided to move back to the country—this time in our own trailer we had purchased, and we placed it behind his parents' house. It seemed like everyone in the country was glad that we were back because we started having house parties, and our house was the place to be where everybody came to hang out and have a good time, and we would go out on the weekends and party because our babysitter lived right in front of us—it was a no-brainer. We could drink and party all night long and stay out as late as we wanted to because my mother-in-law was the sweetest person. She would keep my daughter anytime we wanted to go out. She never said no. When we moved back home, this time it was different. It seemed like we got alone a little better. Oh, maybe because we had our baby, but things were a little calmer than they had been, and there wasn't so many disagreements, fussing, and fighting like there was before.

My husband was working. I was working at the hospital in Opelika at the lab. I became friends with a lady named Matilda. She had been at the hospital working a long time. I mean, I believe this woman could draw blood from a turnip because if you had any blood in your body, she was going to get it. She trained me, and I mean I was trained by the best. I became pretty good at drawing blood. I enjoyed my job. I tried to hide the fact that I was pregnant from my coworkers. I noticed that everyone was always staring at the new girl.

I said to myself, *I believe they know I'm pregnant.* But I still didn't say anything. I always wore big clothing and wore a large lab coat. There was always a smart-ass in the group. Her name was Sara. You would think that she would try to bite your head off, but she really wouldn't. She was nice after you get to know her. She said, "Either you got a watermelon under your shirt, or you pregnant." So the gig is up—everyone knew that I was pregnant. Matilda, my trainer, decided that we would no longer take the elevator. She would not let me get on the elevator to save her life. We walked those stairs daily. She called it walking the baby out of me—meaning, easy delivery of my baby. Luckily, at the time, it was only a three-story hospital. This time, during my pregnancy, I wasn't abused when I went into labor. I went naturally, and I was excited about that.

One morning, as I was getting ready to go to work, I started having pains, and I started to stay at home.

I said it to myself, "You work at the hospital next to labor in delivery." When I got to work, I told my supervisor that I was having pains.

He said, "If the pain intensifies, just walk next door to labor and delivery, and just let me know."

I started having more pain and more pressure and more pain and more pressure, so I told my supervisor I couldn't take the pain any more—labor and delivery, here I come.

The nurses in labor and delivery laughed at me because I was in my uniform. They said, "You came to work and ended up over here. You came to the right place." They checked me out. "Oh, yes, you're in labor."

I called my husband because he worked morning shift as well, and I told him to come to the hospital because I was getting ready to have this baby. When he got to the hospital, he seemed agitated like he didn't want to be there. I was in so much pain, and I didn't feel like hearing anything negative. Of course, him being the devil in sheep's clothing, he looked at me. I'm having all these pains, and this man had the nerve to say, "You need to hurry up because I got to go back to work."

I was shocked. "I'm having your damn baby, and you got the audacity to tell me to hurry the fuck up. If you don't want to be here, you can leave because I can't speed up God's work."

He sat there with this stupid look on his face like, "I know she didn't tell me to leave."

The nerve of this man not to have sympathy for me giving birth to his child, I was thinking. *How crazy on my behalf to still be married to this bipolar, narcissistic person.* I was just stupid—at least that's how I felt.

His father became sick. He was going back and forth to the doctor's office. He was diagnosed with a rare form of leukemia that could be passed to his children or his grandchildren—that was scary to me. He was admitted into Birmingham Hospital, had stayed in the hospital for weeks, and the doctor told them that there was nothing else that they could do for him, that it was only a matter of time before he would pass from his illness.

His father eventually passed from his illness. My baby daughter was about two years old when he passed. When we went to the funeral, my husband didn't cry. He didn't shed a tear. That was strange to me, but when we got home and no one was around, he started crying like a baby. I mean this man cried. I couldn't believe it. I sat beside him on the bed, and I put my arms around him, and I said, "I told you that you loved your father. Go ahead and cry for him because you love him and he loves you, and now he's gone. You always thought that you didn't love him, but deep down inside you really did." I didn't know the man had a heart, and I don't think I ever saw that side of him again.

After his father passed, his mother didn't want to live in their house anymore. She decided to move with her daughter; that left us with a mobile home that we did not know what to do with because we didn't want to live there either. So we rented the mobile home out—the first sign of me becoming an entrepreneur, but at the time I didn't know that. So we moved back to Opelika. I could not believe the neighborhood that we move to, those people that my husband had been friends with at the apartment complex lived down the street from us—the same couple we fought about, which made my baby come early.

I said, "I can't win for losing. Who wants to be neighbors with them again?"

Oh, my husband was happy he had his friend back—his buddy, his running partner in crime. You couldn't hit my husband in the ass with a red apple—he was the man. He would go get dressed, put on his nice clothes that I would buy for him with his money, put on his cologne, and go out with the guy down the street. I knew they were going to meet women; I just couldn't prove it. He was the big man in town. He had gotten a job at Flowers Bakery. The pay was good. Those white uniforms they wore made the guys look good, and the ladies would holler at them when they were outside on break and sometimes stop and talk with them and exchange numbers. Every man wanted to work there because the job paid good. My husband got a big head after landing that job; he thought all the ladies wanted him. Of course, they want you—they think you got lots of money; they are going to come running. He told me one time we should have waited to get married.

I told that fool, "Are you sure you want to get married because I have been married before. Don't jump into something you are not ready for because marriage ties you down." He said he wanted to do it anyway. Careful what you wish for—your wish just might come true. He wasn't ready—not for marriage. We're living in a small subdivision. His aunt lives there also down the street. We would visit them often. His cousin Tim had a friend named Harp. Harp and his girlfriend, Myrna, and her children lived up the road from the subdivision. My husband, Tim, and Harp started hanging out at one another's house. I wasn't included in these get-togethers; they were hanging so tight that one particular hot summer day, my husband came and told me, not asked me like a person who respects his marriage, that Harp and Myrna were going to throw Myrna a birthday party at our house.

I said, "What's wrong with their house? If they want to have a party, they should have it there."

He didn't want to take no for an answer. I told my husband the devil is a liar. "How are you going to tell me that another guy's woman wants to have a party at my house? I don't know these people. They are your friends, and they're not coming here to have a party."

He started defending them even more. "They just want to come here and have a party—what's wrong with that?"

I said, "I tell you what—him or his girlfriend better not show up at this damn house and have a party. I promise you that!"

Guess what—they didn't have a party at my house. I don't know where they had the party, and I didn't care. Hopefully at their own damn house.

So this was when I noticed my husband was sleeping with that girl because, I mean, who in their right mind is going to come home and tell his wife some strangers want to have a party at our house? It didn't make any sense—make it make sense to me because I'm lost. He started to get too close to Harp. I knew something in the milk wasn't clean; this relationship reminded me of the friendship he had with the people at the apartment complex. He said he was working doubles, coming home all different kinds of hours. When I would call his job, they would say he has already left, so I got in detective mode. I started checking his underwear for semen and smelling them for coochie odor. When I would question him about not being at work like he said, that would be a fight. This man was driving me crazy.

One night, after he came home from a party, I noticed a hickey on his neck because I would look at him from head to toe. When I asked him if that was a hickey, he replied, "No, I got bitten by a mosquito."

"So you think I'm a dummy. You are a lying bastard," and that was a fight. I had to call the police like I always did and signed a warrant, and by the time the court date arrived, he begged me not to go to court and promised that it wouldn't happen again. That became a regular cycle for me and him. He would smell like women's perfume and come home with lipstick on his shirts. He was living his life.

One of his cousins told me that Ant asked him if he can use his apartment so he could hang out with some of his lady friends. His cousin said, "I told him no because I got too much respect for you, and I think what he is doing is wrong." Someone actually felt my pain and realized what I was going through. I had no control of what was going on in my life—I was crying. I was staying up all night. I was lost. I was drinking even more. I was slowly becoming an alcoholic. This abuse and disrespect was pushing me to the edge.

As the abuse continued, I thought everything was my fault. I started thinking what I can do to improve our marriage—what can I do to make him happy? How can I satisfy him? The increase in name-calling and degrading was at an all-time high. I came to the realization that it was not me. He didn't love nor respect me because he would often say, "Your family doesn't give a damn about you," and he was right—they don't—that's why you should do everything you can to keep this family together in a loving way, but he doesn't realize that God had given him a wife.

We were having a knockdown drag-out fight.

He told me, "If you get you some business, you won't have time to worry about what I'm doing."

I said, "You are my damn business. You sure in hell aren't spending your time with me, so who are you spending your time with?"

That statement he made would come back to haunt him. I never forgot what he told me. I was truly being a wife and not cheating, but every dog has his day coming, and revenge would be mine.

"You don't want me anymore. You have so many women in this town to choose from. You're bored with me. Nothing is the same. We have two babies."

One night, I drove to my sister's house. I got pissy drunk. I was driving fast with my two children in the car. I was driving fast past the hospital, and I noticed a car rushed up behind me and turned on the blue lights. Damn, it's the police. I was drunk. I pulled in at Checkers Restaurant.

He said, "I pulled you over 'cause you were speeding in a twenty-five miles-per-hour limit. License and registration, please." Then he said, "Have you been drinking?"

I was thinking in my head all I could get.

He said, "Get out of the car, ma'am. I need for you to walk a straight line." After I failed that, he said, "I need you to recite the alphabet."

Now you know damn well I can't do any of that shit right now; I barely made it to D or F. Anyway, he said, "You are under arrest for driving under the influence of alcohol. Do you have anyone that can come get your kids? If not, I will have to call DHR."

It's funny how you can straighten up when your kids are threatened to be taken away. Somehow I got in touch with Ant, and he picked the kids up and bailed me out of jail. That was my very first time being locked behind bars. He joked and laughed about me being arrested for a while. "But you are the reason I'm mentally incapable of controlling my emotions. I'm making irrational decisions—negative outcomes are bound to happen."

My mom was so mad at me. I was getting backlash from everyone, but it was for my own good. Now everyone thinks I'm the family drunk because I would drink too much at my relatives' houses, and they started calling me an alcoholic, which didn't help my self-esteem. I was soaking in sorrow, not feeling love from anyone, thinking maybe God should take me. "I'm not good at anything, I don't have any talents, I'm not loved I'm just breathing air that someone else can use, I'm a nobody, and my husband makes sure I remember that."

Between all this chaos, I got baby number three; I'm guessing I was about six months. He was cheating on me so bad I was losing my mind, but I got these kids. What was I going to do? I could feel that he didn't want me anymore—there were too many fish in the sea, and he just landed in the ocean. I was past frustrated. I was becoming suicidal, having anxiety. I was a hot mess, but I've got to maintain my sanity for my children. I never drank during my pregnancies. I confronted him every day. We were going at it every day. On this day, I guess he really got tired of me, and he slapped me so hard I fell on the floor in the house. I remember lying there. He didn't even pick me up.

My two girls came to me and said, "Mommy, Mommy, are you okay?" This man walked out the house. I was pregnant. He was not showing any concern about me being okay. He went wherever he was going. You can't tell me I wasn't stuck on stupid; I couldn't see the forest for the trees. Why am I here? What am I doing wrong? My self-esteem was at an all-time low.

After I had my son in July, I found a letter to my husband from Myrna—remember, Harp's girlfriend—just what I had suspected all along. Bitch, I got you now. I kept the letter for proof. I wasn't pregnant anymore. I called my sister Carolyn and told her.

She said, "I will go with you to the bitch's house."

When my sister got to my house, I had my bat in my hand, and I said, "Let's go."

Carolyn was always with that shit. I went up to her house, and I confronted her, and I said, "Are you going with my husband?"

She said, "No, he is just friends with my boyfriend."

She looked at that bat, and I looked her straight in her eyes, and I pointed that bat and her face.

I said, "Bitch, when I catch you with my husband, I'm going to kill you."

Never take a threat lightly. The abuse from my husband didn't stop. It was a bad situation for children to be in. Every time I would go up to my mom's house after a fight or argument, they really didn't want us there. She always said, "Make sure you bring some groceries."

Woman, you know I don't have a job. Where will I get some groceries from? Each time I was at her house, I was so uncomfortable, and they made you feel unwanted. My children couldn't eat my sister's children's food. She said, "Y'all need to bring what y'all like to eat." She should have told me that to my face and not my children's. How are you going to tell a child that? So instead of me going to my mother's house when we would fight, I started driving myself and my children to the battered women shelter in Atlanta. Since I had lived there before, I felt more comfortable being in the shelter.

My husband would get in touch with me and tell me, "You shouldn't have those kids all the way in Atlanta in a shelter. You all need to come home. I promise you I will not hit you again, and everything is going to be all right."

I believed that fool, knowing that none of it was true. It was like he knew I didn't have a choice but to come back home to him. He was in control. He was the abuser. He knew how to handle the situation. He knew that I was stuck with him and that he could treat me any way he chose because who was going to rescue me? Who cared what happened to me? He often told me, "Your family doesn't care," even though if I really needed someone, Carolyn was coming, but I believe if my mother would have come and put her input in on what's going on in this marriage, maybe—just maybe—it would have meant something to him.

One night, way across town, on the south side, his cousin was having a party. I didn't go to the party, but something kept telling me to go to the party and check it out. I heard there was going to be a girl there that he dated from my small town. I loaded my children up. My sister Joyce lived across town on the south side as well where the party was. I took my children to her house, and I told her, "I'm going up the street that Ant is at the house party, and I'm going to see what's going on."

I drove up to the house and parked the car. I asked one of his cousins, "Tell Ant that I'm outside." I didn't get out of the car. I was sitting under the steering wheel. I let the passenger side of the window down.

He said, "What you doing here?"

I said, "I just came to see you, what's going on?"

He said, "Nothing. You are not coming to this party."

I said, "What you mean I can't come to this party? Your bitch must be in the house."

He didn't say anything because he knew that girl was in the house. To keep me from seeing this girl, this man grabbed me from the passenger side of the car and pulled me from under the steering wheel and started to beat me right there. His family, they came outside, but no one was trying to get this man off me, and from what I could hear, they were laughing.

Like I said, my sister lived down the road. My nephew Chico was riding past the party, and he saw a man and a woman fighting. He knew I was stopping by the party. He told me that he said to himself, "That looks like my Aunt Cynt." He stopped because there were so many of them. He went and got his posse because my sister Joyce didn't play the radio, and Ant knew that because she told him one day we were at her house, "You wouldn't beat me the way you beat my sister because I would whip your little ass." Ant always told me he wouldn't fight Joyce.

My sister Joyce was so mad when she got there. She was ready to beat Ant's ass herself and told him she would because she had her pistol with her. He knew not to get smart with her. Ant was trying to explain to my sister and calm her down. He knew Joyce's reputation, and the other relatives were saying we didn't have anything to do with it.

"So y'all just going to let this man kill my sister. I keep telling Cynt to leave your ass."

Everybody was looking stupid because my family wanted to fight, but they didn't. I don't remember him coming home that night. This was not my husband—he was a stranger in this house. After this incident, my brother wanted to confront Ant, but my mother told him, "Don't go down to their house and get involved in any of that mess they have going on." My brother and Ant had an altercation earlier on in our relationship; I don't really think my brother wanted to get involved anyway. I can understand where my mom was coming from because sometimes when you involve yourself in other people's relationships, it can lead to someone getting hurt or killed for no reason, and the people who originally had all the fights and disagreements sometimes stay together as if nothing was going on. Why bury a loved one because of other people's problems? So I totally understood where my mother was coming from, but I felt like me being her baby daughter, that she would have been a little more concerned about my safety.

You would think after some of these incidents with my husband that he would say, "Okay, let me try to straighten up because I do have a family that I love. I have a wife. I take care of my family. I am their provider and make sure they got everything that they need. So why can't I settle down and realize that I'm married? Why can't I stop cheating? Why can't I stop disrespecting her and beating her? Why can't I stop doing all these horrible things to her?" If he ever thought about how he treated me, he never showed me any different. If he cared, I couldn't tell. It was the same old, same old thing day after day.

His sister called me one day to ask me, "Who is this girl that Ant has in the car with him at our house?"

I told her, "I don't know—just another girl he is sleeping with."

He couldn't understand there are some people who look down upon what he was doing. He thought he was representing himself as being a king or a man in the streets, but people didn't like what they were seeing. So everything he did, someone always let me know; someone always called to tell me. I even had a man to call me and tell me that his wife was dating my husband and he had purchased her a car.

He said, "Let's do what they're doing."

I told him straight up, "I'm not the person that my husband is. I have respect for myself. But you can tell your wife that she doesn't have herself shit. She is going to hate she messed up her marriage dating him, so don't worry. You have nothing to fear. Have a great day." He never called me back again.

See, the fights and the arguments just continued. It was just like a daily routine. The police were always at our house. I was always signing warrants. I never showed up for court. It was a cycle. I was living in a circle. I was an emotional wreck. I had nowhere to turn and nowhere to go. When you talk about being lost and at the lowest point of your life, it was me living a lie when we did decided to go to church. Sometimes we would have fought before we got there. I didn't even feel comfortable going to church because I knew I was sleeping with the devil, and we were putting on a front for the people at the church. Sometimes I could barely smile or speak to them; I'm pretty sure they wondered, *What's wrong with her? Why is she acting funny?*

But it was none of that; it was me being tormented in my own home, feeling like a captive in my own body, feeling betrayed by the man I married. We need to let God pick our partner because when you are only seeking the flesh, the flesh will fool you. You've got to seek that person who fears God, who loves God, who believes in God, and who has the same values and respect for human beings like you do. We fall short on all the morals and respect that goes along with the relationship because he or she looks good, because he or she is fine. But have you ever stopped to wonder, *Is that person emotionally equipped and ready for the next step in life? Are they ready for the challenges that the world brings? Are they ready to not let the flesh take over because the flesh is weak?*

The body, soul, mind, and spirit are supposed to be strong to resist temptation. You must be strong in your faith in God to sustain yourself in the battles that we go through, which is very hard to do, but you must dig down deep inside to find the strength to resist the temptations of the world. That's why God says we are not of this world. We make living so hard for ourselves without even realizing it. It would have been so easy for him to ask me for a divorce—I've been divorced before—but this time. remember I married for love. I didn't know how to break away from this unhealthy relationship. What would happen to me if I left this man for good? How would I survive? I have never lived in the projects. I have never been on welfare. I got food stamps once while I was married for a year. When it was time for my recertification, I was scared when I sat at that lady desk, and she spoke. "If you are lying about your application, you could receive jail time." I was so scared that I stopped receiving the food stamps. I didn't want to go to jail. After going for that DUI, jail wasn't for me—I would not survive! I was told to work for what I wanted, but in this marriage, I didn't have to work if I didn't want to—the only good thing that I can say is that financially we were taken care of; he went out and made the money. He brought the money home for me to pay the bills. He just didn't want me questioning him on what he was doing or who he was doing it with.

I said "I do, until death do us part." We said we would take care of one another and that we will always be there in sickness and in health. This time when I said those vows, I meant it because I was in love; I think that's why it was so hard for me to let go, to leave and not come back no matter how many times he beat me, no matter how many times he talked about me to my face. He degraded me, belittled me. I stayed. He had control of my mind.

Once he called my mom to come pick me up. He said, "I want you to come pick your daughter up." He talked to her, and after talking to her, she never showed up. When a man calls your mom to come pick you up and you are his wife because he no longer wants you there, why in the hell couldn't I leave?

One afternoon, I got in his car just to go to the store so I could snoop. My discernment kicked in, "Someone has given you a gift." So I wanted to know what his women got him for Christmas. "Seek and you shall find," and I found just what I was looking for—a nice robe for men to lounge around the house. It was in his trunk under his tire. It didn't look cheap.

When I got home, I took the robe in the house, and I said, "I found what your bitch bought you for Christmas. If a cat was a snake, he would have gotten bitten, but you won't wear it," and he kept saying, "A family member gave me that robe."

I said, "If that was true, it would have been under the tree like all of the gifts." No one in this man's family has given him a gift from the time I had been married to him, so that lie wasn't working. I gave that robe to a very nice old councilman in town whom I was friends with and his wife. They both loved the gift I had given him, and they thanked me; but knowing what I know about my husband, I have so many questions for myself. Why I couldn't gather the strength to run like hell and never look back and let the past be the past? But instead, I drove Ant's brand-new car to my sister Carolyn's house and broke every window in the car. I demolished the car. I wanted him to hurt like I was hurting because he was without a car for about three weeks. He loved that car; he would wash it every weekend, getting it clean for his ladies, so now we both were walking.

But he wasn't done with me yet, and I wasn't done with him. We were still a family. We still had children, but when you have had black eyes, been choked, been shot at, and been beaten and stomped on, isn't that enough for anyone to say, "I just can't take it anymore"? But you've got to be abused to understand how women who are being abused stay with their abusers and never leave. Sometimes when you want to leave, it just might be too late; you might be found half dead or maybe even dead.

You've got to understand the mind of a woman or man who's been abused. They can't seem to find their way out of the relationship because you are being put to a test by your abuser. Only the abuser has the key to unlock the darkness inside you, so don't be so quick to say she just could have left him or why she stayed so long. I would have left and gone home to my mother or parents. I would have stayed with friends or other family members. When you don't have that support system, fake family, fake friends saying they'll be there for you, when the shit hits the fan, you're all alone. You must save your own life. Yes, it is very hard to dig deep in your soul to find you again, and only you can do it.

So as I continue to go through this abusive relationship, we move to a new set of apartments—Crooked Creek. We had about fifteen steps to climb, I was sitting on the balcony, chilling. When I looked across to the next set of apartments, it looked like I saw my husband coming out of this girl's apartment. I could spot that head anywhere when he got home. Whichever way he sneaked to the house, it was on—the usual fighting.

"I saw your ass coming from the girl's apartment."

He swore it wasn't him.

I said, "I can't trust your ass nowhere we go."

After always denying having outside relationships, I couldn't figure out why he never wanted me to work, but I had decided to find a job anyway. I was drawing early-morning blood from patients in the nursing homes, and I would bring the blood back to my house for the courier to pick up. But on this morning, my discernment was on high alert. A voice kept saying, "Turn around, go back home."

I kept driving, and this voice said again, "Turn around, go back home. You need to go back home."

I have very strong discernment, so I decided to follow my mind and what was being told to me. So I drove home, got out the car, went up the stairs, put the key in the door, opened it, and I went straight to our bedroom. I could feel a presence there—something wasn't right. I could feel the presence of another person, yet I didn't see anyone. He was lying on his stomach like he was dead asleep.

I said, "Did I wake you up?"

This guy started yawning like he had been asleep for real.

I said to myself, *I'm going to play this game with you because you are about to win an Academy Award about this sleep role.* So I was talking to him as I sat on the bed beside him, then I lay on the bed with him.

He said, "Why didn't you go to work?"

I said, "I just didn't feel like it, so I decided to come back home."

And then I had to think of something to get in the closet because he had his closet, and I had my own closet. It was kind of chilly outside, so I made up a lie.

I said, "Have you seen our matching jackets? I can't find mine."

He said, "I haven't seen it," so I got up, and I went to my closet, and I started to look through my closet for the jacket, knowing I wasn't looking for the jacket; I was looking to see was anyone in my closet.

When I started to walk toward his closet, he started calling my name. "Cynt, don't open that closet." He repeated, "Cynt, don't open the closet. Please don't open that closet."

The gig is up. I opened the closet door, and that bitch Myrna was sitting in the corner, hiding. I immediately jumped on that ass and commenced to beat the hell out of her.

I said, "Didn't I tell you when I found you with my husband I was going to kill your ass!" I dragged her ass out of the closet by her hair and was beating her in her face, and then I decided to choke her. He couldn't get my fingers from around her neck.

He said, "Cynt, don't kill that girl."

"You got the nerve to be in my house." And I started choking her even harder. Her eyes started turning red. He actually had to pry my hands from around her neck. When she got up, she looked at me. He was holding me back. He told her, "Get out of here." She picked up her clothes and ran out the house with nothing but her bra and panties on. I mean I tried to kill her ass like I had said.

Anthony and I fought all day.

"How are you going to be upset with me when you are the one who allowed a bitch to come to our house? The same girl you said you weren't going with the same friend of your cousin—you said you weren't sleeping with his girlfriend."

I tried to tell Harp that they were sleeping around. Oh, he didn't believe me, so I was wondering how he felt when he found out the rumor was true. This is the ultimate betrayal that a spouse can do—letting another person into the couple's world. This was supposed to be our sacred place. Let no man put asunder. At this point, our marriage vows went out the window, and all trust was gone—lie after lie. Anthony's world had started to cave in on him, and he had no explanation for his actions. But he always somehow managed to put the blame on me. Oh, buddy, not this time. I don't think this was the first time he had done this. I think this was the first time his luck failed him. This is an argument that you are not going to win, and he knew it. So he had to act as if he was all distraught. He was talking like a lunatic. I asked him to take me to my mother's house. I secured my son in his car seat because I didn't know what was about to happen to us.

He said, "I'm just going to get it over with. We are going to die today." He kept saying, "We are going to die today."

"I'm tired of this, but you are the problem. You got caught with another woman in our house, something that I would never do— bring a man to your house—so you are that cheap. A hotel was not an option."

He was driving like a bat out of hell. We went up Highway 431 North going toward Lafayette doing at least a hundred miles per hour. I thought if we had an accident, I might not survive. I had this discerning gut feeling telling me to get out of the car. I begged him to let me out of the car. "Please, just let me out of the car."

I don't know why he stopped beside the road, but he let me out of the car. Remember, my son was in the car when I got out of the car. I said, "Thank you, Jesus, just save my son."

I was walking to my brother's house. He lived on this county road. While I was walking, some people stopped, and they were in a van. They looked like the hippie type. I was kind of scared to get in the van with them, but they were so nice, and they were talking about God. The mother read a scripture to me. I wasn't scared anymore.

They asked me where I was headed and why I was crying. I said I was on my way to my brother's house, off County Road 12, about a half mile up the road. I told them what had happened and that I was afraid that my husband would kill me in a car accident.

They said, "Don't worry. We will take you where you need to go."

These people took me where I asked them to take me, and they dropped me off. I was so grateful. They were really the religious people that they said they were. My brother drove me to my mom's house.

When I got to my mom's house, my sister Carolyn told me that Ant had a car accident with the baby in the car.

I knew it was going to happen. They took me to the accident scene.

All I could say as we drove was, "Lord Jesus, please let my baby be okay. Please, Lord."

When we got there, my baby was sitting in his car seat in the grass. I said, "Thank you, Jesus." I didn't give a damn what happened to Ant just as long as my son was okay. I got my son out of his car seat, and I hugged him with everything within me. God saved my son like I asked him to. God knew that we didn't deserve to die because of Ant's foolishness.

I did go back to the apartment complex where we lived because I wasn't satisfied Ant crossed the line; I wanted to fight him some more. "What were you thinking about? How could you do this to me?" The next day, I was still angry. I decided to go to my sister

Joyce's house. She knew what had happened. We discussed the ordeal for a few minutes, and when I asked her for her pistol, she didn't ask any questions. One of my nephews, young at the time, wanted to ride with me. When we approached the corner of the apartment building, I spotted Myra on her front porch. She had a crowd of people outside. I told my nephew to stay in the car. I parked down the street, got out of the car, and crouched down like the police. I weaved through the cars, and as I got closer to Myra's house, I started shooting. I was shooting at her ass, and people were screaming and running. She knew it was me who did the shooting that day. She knew I wanted to make good on my promise to kill her. But luckily, I didn't. Neither Myra nor Anthony were worth my freedom, and I'm glad that innocent people didn't get hurt that day.

After the police didn't show up at my front door, I knew Myra didn't sign a warrant on me. I knew no one got shot that day, but that would be my final warning to her. And she knew it. I told myself that whenever I saw her, I was going to make her life a living hell. Later that night, we were still arguing about the situation, and our three children were in the house. I remember the front door was open, and I was standing in the doorway. This time I wanted him dead.

I told him, "Bitch, I'm going to kill you. I'm sick of you."

I pulled the gun out of my pocket and lifted it up at him. He knew I was going to use it. My baby was sitting on the floor next to him, so he grabbed my baby and used him as a shield. He launched himself toward me with our baby in his arms. Everything happened so quick. He put the baby down so fast when he reached me, we began to tussle over the gun, and a bullet was discharged in the air. Somehow I lost my balance through the struggle and fell down fifteen steps. When I landed at the bottom, on the ground, I tried to stand up. But upon standing, my right foot went to the right, and my bone pooped out. I fell to the ground, and this enormous pain rushed to my head. I had never experienced so much pain. I said, "Lord Jesus." I was digging in the ground with my fingernails for relief. No matter how much I screamed, no matter how deep I dug in the ground, this was the most excruciating pain I had ever experienced in my life.

Ant said, "The police and the ambulance are on the way," and Ant kept asking me, "Where's the gun?" I didn't care about the gun 'cause the pain was unbearable. He was saying, "I don't want the police to find the gun." Once the ambulance arrived, I was loaded in. I can remember the paramedic saying, "She's going into shock," and I believe they rushed me to the hospital. They x-rayed and cleaned my leg to keep me from having an infection. There wasn't a surgeon on staff that night who specialized in orthopedic surgery, so I was sent home in a cast up to my thigh until a specialist was found.

Once a surgeon was found, I received a call to come to his office. I was waiting for the doctor to come in the room, and when the doctor sat down, he looked worried and began to tell me that he couldn't guarantee me that he could repair my leg because of the way both bones were broken. I was trying to process this devastating news. I said, "Doctor, please, you've got to fix my leg. I have three children at home. I've got to walk again." He said he would try his best.

Leaving the doctor's office not feeling any better than before I arrived was discouraging, but my faith in God said, "I'm not accepting that. You're a doctor, and God will help you repair my leg."

When I arrived at the hospital for my surgery, I didn't have any doubt that the doctor couldn't repair my leg. After surgery, the doctor came to my room and said, "The surgery was a success, but you have a long road ahead of you."

I said, "Thank you, Doctor." I lay in that hospital bed, and I was in so much pain that they gave me morphine to relieve it. Morphine puts you in a different place. I enjoyed when it was time to receive a shot of morphine, and I had started to beg the nurse for more morphine. I was becoming addicted to the medicine because it was the only medicine that would relieve the pain. When I was released from the hospital, I was in a cast from my upper thigh to the bottom of my foot, with only my toes sticking out. I wore this for eight months. It was horrible. Then for two months, I wore a boot.

My doctor was amazed with how my bones healed. He placed a plate with six screws in my leg, which would remain there for the rest of my life. I had to go to therapy to learn how to walk again and apply pressure to my leg. It took me a while to graduate from therapy, but I did. I still had to wear the boot occasionally because walking without the boot was difficult. It took me two years to regain the leg mobility that I had before the accident.

When I would look at my leg, it reminded me of what happened and the abuse I suffered from being married to a monster. It made me sick to my stomach.

But I still couldn't leave him; I was addicted to the abuse syndrome. Girl, you almost lost your life. So what are you going to do, talk in third person? Nothing, absolutely nothing—no matter how many times this man degraded me and beat me in front of my family and his family, I stayed. I didn't think I would ever get the courage to leave. After all that had happened, my husband had a house built for us on Marion Avenue in Opelika. New house, same old shit. Nothing had changed, just a home address.

But I was ready for change. I had gotten a new job at the county shop in Lafayette. I work four days a week, and I would be off on Fridays—we call that a long weekend. When at the county shop, I noticed that the police would ride through there every morning. We worked on Sheriff Department cars, not the city police cars. So one morning, I had arrived at work, and someone entered the building. I was sitting at my desk. Remember, I had never cheated on my husband throughout the whole time we were together through all of that abuse that I endured. I stayed loyal and faithful. But when this chocolate, fine, built-like-a-brick-house man walked in my office with that police uniform on and he said, "You work here now?"

I said, "Yes."

He said, "Okay, I'm going to check on you every morning."

I said, "Okay."

When he walked out that door, I said, "That motherfucker's fine as wine." Boy I couldn't get this dude off my mind. I called one of my girlfriends. I told her about the police officer I met and how fine his body was.

I said, "I'm going to ask him out for lunch."

She said, "All he can say is yes or no."

I said, "I know, right?"

So every day at my lunchtime, I would pick up the phone at my office, and when someone answered, I would hang up. If I wasn't doing that, I was picking up the phone and hanging it up. I know I did this for about a week. I had to build my nerves up to ask him. One day I said, "What the hell—I'm going to ask him." I made the phone call to the police station.

I said, "May I speak to Officer Jones?"

He said, "This is Officer Jones. How can I help you?"

My heart just dropped to the floor. I said, "This is Cynthia, the lady that works at the county shop."

He said, "I know you."

I said, "Would you like to go out to lunch with me?"

He said, "Of course."

My panties got wet right then and there. We started meeting for lunch. Sometimes we will walk all the way up that road from the county shop because not a lot of people travel that road, and sometimes we would go to his house for lunch. I was cheating—it felt great. Remember, Ant told me, "Find you something to do so you won't worry about what I'm doing." Baby, that's the truth—I found me something to do, and guess what, I didn't worry about him at all. Cheating was the answer—yes, it was. This guy treated me nice. He listened to me at the time. He just seemed like the one. Then I thought finally—what do the old folks say?—"Don't count your chickens before your eggs hatch."

We were having a rendezvous; I was meeting him at the park, meeting on dirt roads. We were at old schools that were closed. We were doing it all and having us some good old sex. My husband started to get suspicious. I started coming home late from work. I had a new attitude. I had a new walk about myself, and he was wondering what the hell was going on with this girl. I started lying about where I was going. I started going to the gym. I would just come up with anything to get out of the house so I could go meet my friend. Now I know why my husband was cheating—because it's so damn exciting. Maybe so exciting for me because I was a housewife and my life was boring. Now I got me something to do. So when I got into an altercation at my job with a person, I quit because I know my temper. I didn't want to go to jail for hitting anyone, so I quit. Now I'm back at home every day, once again being that housewife.

My sister Carolyn and my mom would come to visit me at my home. This one particular day, this visit would change my life forever. Everyone must find God at their own time. I started having the desire to get to know God. I finally figured out that was what was missing from my life. I would talk to my neighbor about God, and she would give me scriptures to read. I started praying and worshipping. I could feel that I was having a connection with God. I would read my Bible all the time. I kept my Bible open on my kitchen table, so as I did my house chores, I would take a break and sit down and read the Bible.

My mom noticed when she would stop by my house I was always reading the Bible, so she said to me one day, "What are you trying to do, become one of those sanctified people?"

I just looked at her and said, "I have a soul to save," and I didn't let her antics stop my praise like I did when I was a child. There was something to this prayer thing, and I was not letting go.

How did I open my business? It seemed as if God himself sent my mother and my sister to visit me on this beautiful sunny afternoon. The sun was shining so bright. It was 1997 or 1998. We were sitting on my patio in the back of the house, just talking mainly about me quitting the job at the county shop. I remembered so well because my sister Joyce had been released from prison that year. When she got out of prison, she told us that she had been diagnosed with breast cancer. My favorite sister—I could go to her house anytime I wanted to, and she was always protecting me, but back to the message at hand about the business. I truly believe that this message was sent to me from God through Carolyn. She said, "Have you heard about people opening up home day care?"

I said, "No."

She said, "All you have to do is keep six kids at your house and get paid $1,200 a month. Keep them five days a week. That will be your own business."

I said, "It sounds good," but I like to keep my house clean, and I didn't want anyone's kids at my house every day. I don't want to keep my own badass kids—you know I don't want to keep anyone else's kids. I don't have the patience, so no, I don't want to do it. I felt like I had a calling on my life. I could not shake this feeling of owning a home day care for nothing, I couldn't get it out of my mind. It wasn't about the money even though I knew this would give me a chance for independence from my husband having to give me money, but this feeling was like God wanted me to do this and I must do this.

I couldn't stop the images of me being an abused spouse. What if he gets mad at me while I have these people's kids in our home? Then I thought maybe the abuse will stop because the kids are here. Once my husband got home from work, I told him about the idea that my sister told me about.

He said, "Whatever you want to do, I'm going to back you 100 percent." He asked me questions.

I told him, "I don't know much about it, but I can pick up an orange book from DHR which has all of the details."

So the next day, I went to the DHR building and picked up the book, read up on everything that I needed. I didn't tell my mother or my sister or anyone that I was now interested in becoming a business owner; my husband put my fence up. My aunt and I went every Saturday to the yard sales, and I would purchase the toys that I needed. My aunt helped me set my rooms up. After I passed inspection, I decided to tell my family that I had opened a home day care. At first, Carolyn seemed happy that I had taken her advice and decided to open the home day care. She even told me that I could have the outside toys at her house because her boys weren't playing with any of them, and she told me the day to come pick the toys up. I was excited about her giving me the outside equipment, so I drove to Camphill, where she lived, got out my Tahoe.

I knocked on the door. When she came to the door, I could feel her energy and spirit. She was in a totally different space from when she promised me the toys, so I sat around. I didn't know if I should ask her or not because of the vibe I was picking up on; I was waiting for her to say, "Okay, let's go outside and put the toys inside your truck."

I clearly saw that she was not in the giving mood that I was hoping for, so I said, "Where are the toys you said I could have?"

She gave me a look like she could choke me right there. She said, "You are just like my friend Annie, always want somebody to give you something."

I gasped. I couldn't believe what I was hearing. I stood up, and I told her, "I didn't ask you for anything. I'm going by what you promised me. You said I could have the toys that your boys weren't playing with, but don't worry, keep them. Just don't ever tell me a lie again." I was hotter than a six shooter, and I never asked her for anything again.

Carolyn clearly wasn't happy about giving me the idea to open a home day care, an opportunity she volunteered to disclose to me. I didn't ask for the information, but now she was mad. Carolyn had received her breast implant money from her lawsuit. She didn't share her money with us like she said she would. She had enough money to start her own home day care business or her own center if that's what she wanted to do; she didn't have to tell me anything.

"No, I don't understand why you are mad at this point. And why would you treat me like this?" I got to think about myself and about my family about some things that I want in life, about making a mark in this world for myself, for my children to be proud of me and something that I can leave behind for them. I was hoping, for once in my life, that my mother would be proud of me. When I found out that my mother was just as upset with me as my sister, I was heartbroken. I truly believed this was what divided and destroyed my relationship with my family, and a family feud would begin.

My husband was still abusing me, and he started to do it in front of the day care kids. I had to provide safety for these children, and that's what I was going to do—protect these kids, my children, and myself so I didn't want to leave my home. I really enjoyed working from home. I wanted to even expand into a group home, and I wouldn't have to go out and pay rent on a building, but my husband was not going to act like a normal man and allow me to do my business.

My business was open. I was starting to feel independent of my husband, not having to ask him for money because when he would get mad at me, he would take away all the money, the credit cards, and I would have nothing until he decided to give them back to me. This time I had my own credit cards. I had my own money. I didn't need to ask him for anything. I believe he started to feel jealous and threatened, feeling like he was losing control of me after all this time.

I started out with six kids. As my business flourished as people heard about my home day care center, I started to enroll more children. Then I had twelve kids. I started to enroll after-school children at my home, which allowed me to purchase my first van so that I could pick up kids from school, and I ended up with twenty-four kids in my home, but I had to show where a child was leaving the day care home and being replaced by a child coming in so I wouldn't be over the limit that the state allowed.

As my business flourished, I had operated out of my home for a year. I started to look for a building, and I found my first building on Frederick Road, and I named my center Tiny Tots Daycare. I started with the children that were attending my home day care. I had an open-house party to increase enrollment as business was slow. My name had to spread in the community, and that meant while I was still seeing my friend, it was not as often as I used to because of my work schedule. I had to open the building. I had to cook the meals, go home, get some rest, come back and drive the school pickup route, and stay until my business closed. When you own a business, you have to be prepared to do multiple jobs. My day care opened at 8:00 a.m. and closed at 11:30 p.m. Sometimes I would be so tried that when I would lay the children down at 7:30 p.m. for nap time, I would grab me a cot also and fall asleep with the children.

It wasn't easy. I barely saw my children unless I decided to let them come to the day care after school with me. Thank God I had a good landlord who worked with me because a lot of times I wouldn't have all of my rent money. I wouldn't have all the money to pay the bills. I needed to pay my workers a fair wage, but they stuck with me. I would go in my office and pray and cry daily. I didn't know if I was going to make it.

One day, while I was in my office praying and crying, one of my employees heard me. She knocked on the door. I tried to wipe the tears from my eyes.

She said, "Miss Cynthia, I heard you crying. Everything is going to be all right. God hears your cry," and she gave me a hug.

She made me feel better, and without noticing, before I knew it, my building was full of kids. I was able to pay my staff. I could pay my rent, but the building was getting too small. I didn't realize my husband was so suspicious of my whereabouts because I hired more staff members which freed up time for me, and he also had a new job with Uniroyal Tire Company, so I was sure he had more ladies in his life, but that didn't bother me anymore because I had a friend who showed interest in me, and we spent time together; we went out in public, to clubs, and he introduced me to his family, and my children got to know him.

When I tell you my husband started to become a detective, you know people can't keep a secret. Everyone knew I was dating the police officer including my husband. I would even call my friend while I was sitting in the room with my husband. Stella got her groove back and grew some balls. Payback is a motherfucker. You had the nerve to have a woman in our bed. You can't tell me which side of the road to cross. I guess he realized he had feelings for me or he wanted to prove he wasn't going to be cheated on. Either way, I didn't care, and I was getting some dick too.

Ant was out of control. He had a private detective follow me. When that didn't work, he bugged our house, which I didn't know, but every time I got on the house phone, it would start making a funny-sounding noise, so I told my niece / best friend Toya.

I said, "Do you hear that noise? I believe this phone is bugged."

She said, "It might be because he is trying to keep up with you now."

I said, "Since he listening to my damn conversation, let's give him something to listen to."

I started talking about my friend on every call to her; we were having a ball. I didn't know this idiot was gathering information so he could try to take my children and prove me of being an adulteress and an unfit mother until one day I told Sarah, who started working for me at my home day care.

I said, "I'm tired. I'm going home for lunch and take a nap."
She said, "Okay."

When I arrived home, I went in the house and sat down in the recliner, which was right in front of the TV. Ant started cussing at me, calling me all sorts of names, saying, "Motherfucker, I got you now. I'm going to destroy you. I know all about your boyfriend," but what got my attention the most was that after he ironed his clothes and got dressed, he threw a duffel bag at my feet, and it was open, and it had so many cassette tapes in it, and he said, "I dare you to get it. I want you to try and get it."

Desperate times calls for desperate actions. I kept looking at that bag. I wanted to get my hands on it so bad, but I knew if I didn't have a way to protect myself, I wouldn't remain alive that day, so I started to turn the TV from one investigation show to the next. I was psyching myself out. I kept going in the kitchen. trying to decide which knife I was going to kill him with. I would get one, place it under my thigh. When I sat down, I would say, "This one is too big," because I remembered one time in his cousin's house I tried to cut him with a razor, and he took the razor and cut the inside of my hand open and laughed about it. I kept asking his cousin to take me to the emergency room, and he took his time; so I knew if I'm going to do this, I better make it count.

I went into my living room, got on my knees, and I said, "Lord, forgive me for what I'm about to do. Today is the day that I'm going to kill him. I can't take it anymore, and I'm not letting him take my children. In Jesus's name, amen."

I got up, went to the kitchen one last time, and got the perfect knife. I said to myself, "Bitch, if you don't kill him, he is going to take this knife and kill you."

After I said that, I had no fear inside me. I had made up my mind—he was going to die today. I placed the knife under my thigh. He kept prancing around, like, yep, I got her ass.

He said, "This is what you want, don't you? Come and get it."

He was continuing to torment me. He reached down and picked the bag up and started to walk toward the front door. I got up out of that chair, and I reached back with all my strength, and I stabbed him in the back, but at that moment, I felt something or someone grab me and wouldn't let me stab him. Again, it's like God stepped in.

Ant turned around. He looked at me with fear in his eyes, and he said, "Cynt, you stabbed me." He was shocked and bleeding.

I said, "Naw, motherfucker, I'm going to kill you. We are going to die today—that's what you want, isn't it?" I could feel my eyes dancing back and forth. I had never seen so much fear in his eyes. He didn't know what to do.

"If you come toward me, today will be the day we die."

He was so scared he dropped the bag—all his evidence he had against me. He went out into the front yard and started screaming, "She stabbed me! Someone call the ambulance and the police!"

I grabbed the bag of cassette tapes, got in my car, and I met the police as I was driving to the police station. I drove into the police station park, opened the door, and was surrounded by police. They were saying, "Where is the knife, ma'am?"

I said, "It's on the front seat." They cuffed me and put the knife in a plastic bag. I kept telling the officers to look his name up because he has multiple domestic violence complaints. I was booked. I was supposed to stay twelve hours, but they let my mom bail me out in two hours and said, "The judge is releasing you." That's when you know God is in the midst of it all. So when we went to court, he had an attorney; I didn't. Just myself and God walked in that courtroom.

When they called our case up, the judge said, "Mrs. Peavey, you got tried, didn't you?"

I said, "Yes, sir, I did."

The judge said, "Case dismissed."

Ant moved out the house. I was scared to live with him after that, but for some reason, he didn't want to give me a divorce. He stopped paying on the house we had built, and I didn't pay on it either. I went and purchased myself two acres of land and moved a trailer on it. In the middle of all this chaos, we were already in our new building across town. This building was larger. Everything was going good. I even increased my staff members. I had enrolled even more children. We were happy. We did a local commercial about my day care center with the local television station. I don't know if this brought the haters out of the woodwork, but I regretted doing that commercial.

Working with those children and their families was the only job that I had ever committed myself to. I loved those children and would do anything for them. Their parents knew they could trust me and my staff with their children while in our care. I had a parent with a disabled child. He was a full-time student with me until he became sporadic. His mother enrolled him in a school for handicapped children. Even though he had started coming to us occasionally, we knew his habits. We knew what he liked and what he didn't like, and we also knew that he was a very happy child, that he never became sick in our care. He had come home to visit and stay with his family for two weeks, so that also meant that he would be in my care for those two weeks while his mother worked. She was a single mom that worked daily to provide for her children, and she was a sweet person. She always had a smile on her face, and she loved her kids.

We all encounter hard times. We all go through difficulties, and challenges come in our lives. We don't always make good decisions— we all are guilty of it. We kept Jason in a high chair so that the other children wouldn't hurt him, but he wouldn't be in the high chair all day; it was just a precaution used. On this visit, something was different about him. He wasn't playing, laughing; he just wanted to sleep. His teacher noticed the difference in his behavior and reported to me the situation. After observing him a couple of days and a spike in his temperature, I called his mom on her job, and I informed her that she would have to pick Jason up. She came right on to pick him up. We discussed with her our concerns about him being sick. I advised her to take Jason to the doctor the next day and that he couldn't return without a doctor's excuse. She wasn't happy about what we discussed, and she informed me that staying out of work would be a problem. She kept telling me she couldn't get off work like that, and I explained to her, "Please just do it for your child," and I thought we had a clear understanding of the situation at hand—his health. The next morning, I was awakened by a phone call from my cook.

She was hysterical. She was breathing heavily. She was screaming my name.

"Miss Cynthia, Miss Cynthia, Jason has collapsed on the floor."

I said in disbelief, "He wasn't supposed to be at the center. Did she leave a doctor's excuse?"

She said no.

I said, "Is he breathing?"

She said, "I don't think so."

I couldn't believe what I was hearing. I said, "Call 911, and get Justine to perform CPR."

My cook replied, "Okay," and she said, "Justine is already doing CPR."

I was living twenty minutes away at that time—I think I made it in ten minutes. When I arrived at the center, they were loading Jason into the ambulance.

One of the paramedics pulled me to the side and said, "Your worker was performing CPR when we arrived. That helped save him."

I was about to lose my mind. I asked my cook, "Did you tell her that he couldn't stay at the center?"

She said, "Yes, we did, but she told me to tell you that she couldn't lose her damn job, and she sat him in the middle of the floor."

No one knows the feeling that was going through my body at the time—the uncertainty of his condition, not knowing why she would disobey the rules of the center and why she would jeopardize her child's life. I know it wasn't intentional because she loved him; I think the stress of providing for her children led to her making an uninformed decision. Sometimes you have to do what you have to do, but in the midst of that, it was jeopardizing me at the same time.

About 10:00 a.m., I got a call from the doctor at the ER. She told me that the child died. I couldn't believe what I was hearing. I was crying. I was so hurt inside.

The doctor said, "It was nothing that you all did wrong. He had pneumonia in his lungs. His lungs were so black that we couldn't save him."

Two DHR workers came to the center about lunchtime, and they told me that they had spoken to the doctor, and if I wanted to close for the rest of the day, I could and reopen the next morning. But the street committee had spread the story like wildfire. The local news station was all over the story. My center was on the news. People can be so cruel—they were spreading all sorts of lies all over town in the surrounding areas. Other day care owners were telling parents not to enroll their children with me because we had killed a kid; we had thrown a kid on the wall, and he died. It was awful. People didn't know if they wanted him to be an infant or a six-year-old.

I spoke to Jason's mother on the phone, and she said, "So many people were telling me to sue you."

I paused, and I gathered my composure, and I said, "You do what you got to do because I know what the doctor told me he died of." I held my head up high and remained open. My business suffered. I lost clients because of this incident—people not having the knowledge of what happened and just listening to lies. I had to lay off some staff and fight the ugly rumors. When someone stopped by, the first thing they asked was about the incident that had occurred, so I had to go in prayer, step back, and let God take control.

It took a while for me to regain the trust of the people, but slowly I did, but every once in a while, someone would remind you of an incident that you have buried. So as my business started to flourish again, everything was going good because anything can happen at any time in day care; it is an unpredictable business, and safety is the key. The lady whose child died at the hospital's other two children remained at my center. She knew the truth, and we remained friends.

My enrollment was up. Remember, what man meant for bad, God will always turn it into good. After reclaiming my good name, not a lot went on that was out of the ordinary. The center was in front of the post office and an employment service; I couldn't understand how they would have time to do their job and watch the children on the playground at the same time. They were always reporting to DHR incidents that occurred on the playground. They wouldn't give me a chance to do my job. It really became a pain in the butt, so

I went and confronted both businesses, and I told them to keep their nose in their own business and not worry about what's going on at Tiny Tots Daycare.

I didn't have any more trouble out of them, but if you are in the business of keeping children, something is bound to happen, and you can't please all parents, and you lose some children to other day cares along the way. My children and I were living in this old trailer that I paid cash for on my two acres of land. It was in the country, and it was scary at nighttime, but I had to be brave for my children. I slept on the sofa, and I let my children have the beds. People just don't know your trials and tribulations. We went from a nice four-bedroom home to a raggedy trailer. When I started to see lizards inside the trailer, I didn't know how long I could stay there, but we managed. I would gather my children up, and we would kneel in the middle of the floor, and we would pray. I wanted them to learn to worship God regardless of their situation.

I had enrolled more after-school kids who needed to be taken to school. I hired two extra van drivers to accommodate the number of children I had enrolled. I went to my mother to get her to help me purchase a new van. I needed a cosigner after convincing her that I would make my payments on time each month because she really didn't want to help purchase this van. I told her she didn't have to worry about anything because I'm a woman that keeps her word, and she taught me that your word is your bond.

I was a proud owner of a 2000 Chevrolet fifteen-passenger van—my first brand-new van, not used. My driver was enjoying this van; it looked good. I was proud to be a business owner and thankful for the things that I had accomplished through the grace of God.

I was awakened once again early in the morning. When you are awakened out of your sleep, your thoughts are foggy, and you are trying to get yourself together. The caller said, "Is this Cynthia Peavey? Do you own Tiny Tots Daycare? This is an officer from Opelika Police Department."

I said yes in my subconscious mind.

She said, "Your van is on fire, and we need you to come down here."

I said, "That's a brand-new van. It's not on fire," and I hung up the phone because I thought it was someone playing on the phone, so I was going to go back to sleep.

The phone rang again. This time the officer said, "This is Opelika Police Department. Mrs. Peavey, don't hang this phone up. Your van is on fire, and you need to come to your day care as soon as possible."

I knew at that moment this was not a joke. I got to the day care as fast as I could. I could see the van burning as I turned the corner to approach the building. I got out the car. I fell to the ground, and I was screaming and crying, "Not my van, God, why? Why would someone do this to me? What have I done to deserve this kind of punishment? Why would someone hate me so much?"

I asked the officer, "Can y'all find out who did this?"

He said, "It would be hard because it was burned completely up, so someone used gasoline."

This was a message to me, and it was a deliberate act. I couldn't understand the lack of empathy for my business and for the kids enrolled at my center. I started thinking, *Would my sister have this done because she was in competition with me and didn't like the fact that our mother helped me get this van, or was it someone who was jealous of my success?* I would never know who did this cruel act and what was the reason behind it, but my faith in God tells me that they paid dearly for that act.

After that, I had to go and purchase an old van once again. At the time, my mother was working for my sister Carolyn. I wanted my mom to ask me, "Baby, do you need for me to come help you out sometimes too?" but we don't always get what we ask for, then sometimes I think maybe she was waiting on me to ask, but I knew how selfish my sister had become; I didn't want to stir the fire.

Don't look from the outside of any family and think that they are perfect; everyone has skeletons in their closet. So my children's father finally gave me a divorce. He fought against it as long as he could, and he finally said okay. Ant knew that I was seeing Bobby, but he didn't have a clue that we were planning to get married. So when he found out that I was married, he went off on me big time, and I was afraid to be around him because I didn't know what he was going to do. He wanted to kill me. I couldn't understand how he was going around town, telling everyone that the failure of the marriage was my fault because I cheated. I don't know if this was his tactic on how he was going to get women, or had he just plain out lost his mind?

"Man, you treat me like garbage. You said that I would never become shit, that I never would have shit, and that I didn't come from shit and that nobody wants me. Everything you ever told me negative, God made you out to be a liar and showed you that someone loves me now. Let that marinate in your spirit."

When I first met Bobby, I was in this horrible marriage. I was verbally being abused. I was being neglected. I was being physically abused and mentally abused. It was nice to meet a man who thought that I was somebody, who treated me like I was a human being, who liked being around me, who didn't talk bad about me, who didn't belittle me, and he didn't drink a lot of alcohol. He was a breath of fresh air, and I was about to breathe in deep, baby! Coming out of the relationship that I came out of, I brought baggage with me. When he met me, he didn't know that Cynthia was the calm, withdrawn person that took all of the abuse and that my alter ego, Cindy, she's that bitch that didn't take shit from anybody. Cindy enjoyed drinking and partying, I started to realize that people who have been abused sometimes become abusers.

I started to slow down. I tried to keep Cindy hidden; that's why I would try to limit my alcohol intake and wanting to go to clubs because she was going to show up, and he didn't like to go out to clubs. We did more eating out and hanging out with his family. I'm trying to impress this man. He doesn't need to know all my bad habits because, baby, he might say *no*.

He was in the middle of a divorce. We were trying to heal at the same time. I thought, *Maybe this time I'm getting it right. For the first time.* They say three time's a charm.

I do say that sometimes we don't realize the difference between love and lust, and I thought after five years of dating, I knew the difference. I really, really tried to make it work. When I'm in a relationship, I take that commitment to heart. I'm not a cheater unless you push me to that level. I didn't want my insecurities, my baggage to interfere with this relationship. You can date a person for twenty years and still don't know if they are truly your soulmate. The vows that you take for better or for worse, in sickness and in health, until death do us part—do we really mean that? Are we really going to stand by those vows? When I'm sick, are you going to stand by my side? When the worst happens to me, are you going to be there with me to hold my hand and tell me everything's going to be all right and stay with me no matter how bad the situation is? Or will you just walk away? Are you only there for the good times? Are you only there for financial gain? Will you leave when the money is gone? Will you help me rebuild myself when I'm down and out? Will you be there when the pain is so bad that I think suicide is the answer? Or will you just walk away like a coward because your reputation is in jeopardy, ashamed of being associated with the person that you told God you'd love?

I came to realize that this third marriage that I'm about to get into will break down a wall in my life that I wasn't even expecting, and my business would put me on a path of destruction that I didn't see coming, that my life would change in a blink of an eye, that the devil would descend upon me and I would have the fight of my life to choose between good and evil. Would my faith stand the test of time through all of my trust, faith, and belief in God? I would have to prove it like God was saying, "I see you, my warrior, but my warriors have battles that they must conquer, and you, my child, it's time for your test. You say you love me, but you have never seen me. You say you trust me, you say you have faith in me, and you say you want to live with me in my kingdom. I want you to pass this test. Whatever you do, my child, don't let go of my unchanging hands."

Then he said, "Devil, do to her as you wish, but don't take her life, and at the end she will come to me."

You never know why God is doing what he is doing, but it is for a reason even though we don't understand that reason. I bet you it's to elevate you to the next level of your life; it's to make you a better person. Everyone is not meant to go where God have planned for you, but this did cause me to rethink everything I had ever known about life.

Every man is different. Every woman is different. The challenges we face are going to be different. People's beliefs are different. Some people have good traits. Some people have bad traits. No one is perfect. Don't ever believe that the unbelievable could not happen to you. Anything can happen to anyone at any point in time in their life, no matter how good of a person you are, no matter how much you give to other people, no matter how much you sacrifice. What you want and how you feel for other people, people don't consider your feelings. Everyone is out for themselves. No one could have told me that this would be mistake number three or that I would have a life without walls.

When our house was being built, I would go by there every day. Once I get off work from the day care center, I would stop at the site where our house was being built just to make sure that everything was going like it was supposed to—hey, I was excited. This was my second house being built, but it was still exciting to watch the walls go up, to watch the floors being put in, to watch the sheetrock being put on the studs, and to go in; and they painted the walls, the fixtures were in place, and the toilets were set. Then you get a move-in date, and that's the happiest time of your life. I was moving in a new home with the new husband, with my children. We were moving in the month of November, right before Thanksgiving, my favorite time of the year. I was anxious, excited, ready to move. My husband, Bobby, and I and my children were living in a two-bedroom house in his hometown, so, you know, I was more than ready to move out of that house.

We had the trailer pulled into a trailer park in Opelika and rented it out, and that was 2003. That was my second mobile home that I had rented out.

When I told my husband I was going to go ahead and move my clothes and my kids' clothes down to the house, I said, "When are you going to bring yours?"

He said, "I'm not going to move right now because of my job," and I was thinking in my head, *Because of your job—you're only a police officer. You don't work seven days a week, so you've got plenty of time to move your clothes.*

So I figured I would help him out. I said, "I can move your clothes when I move mine."

He said, "No, you don't have to do that."

But naw, I'm hardheaded. I got my brother to help me move his clothes into our new home. After I did that, when he came down, he wasn't happy and said, "I told you not to move my clothes. I know when I want to move down here."

So I kind of brushed it off, and I said, "I don't know why you wouldn't want your clothes here. Do you plan to move here?" You know it was only going to take him about fifteen minutes to get to work from where we live, so I was like, *This man been all around the world while he was in the Army, and now you want to have small-town withdrawals. Boy, I really know how to pick a man. What in the hell is he talking about?*

After we had been living there for a while, I noticed he never asked, "Hey, bae, what bill came out this month?" I thought maybe he just overlooked the light bill on the table, so I took him the light bill in front of his brother who was there visiting. He told me he didn't have the money. Why would this man tell me he doesn't have the money for the light bill? You know I was getting upset now. I didn't want to act a fool in front of his brother. I waited for his brother to leave, and I started a huge argument about "Are you going to pay this light bill? 'Cause I'm wondering now, did you marry me because you love me, or did you marry me because I have a day care center and you think I got some money?"

I told him, "I tell you what—my kids better not ever be in the dark, and they better always have cable. So that's why you weren't ready to move in." That's when I should have left his ass in his hometown because it was a big deal to me; maybe it wasn't to him. But I bet you after that, he paid the light bill and the cable because I wasn't playing, and I meant what I said.

You ready now for the real me to come out because, you know, she had been hiding, trying to be a good girl. But you really don't want to start an argument with me unless you are able to hang with the big dogs. As time passed, I was being a mom, a dad, a boss, came home and cook dinner, made sure my kids were straight. And in the meanwhile, I was hearing all kinds of rumors about him being a womanizer while working on the police force, both of our phones were on the same bill. When the phone bill would come in the mail, of course, I would open it and scale all the numbers especially if he spent a lot of minutes talking to this one number—that's how I caught him having an affair while on duty. He had been on the phone with this lady for hours, and it was happening on numerous occasions. I should have been a detective because I called her to first see if a woman would answer the phone, then I got her address, and guess what? I showed up on her doorstep—yes, in the flesh. If I'm going to be faithful to you, at least you could return the favor. So now I've got one that doesn't abuse me, but you can't keep them eyes and hands to yourself. I'm not going through this again.

He denied and denied having a relationship with this woman. After he knew I was not buying his story, now it was a different story. First lie, "I let my nephew use my phone," so I called the nephew. I think I got to speak to the nephew before he did, and the nephew told me he hasn't used his phone. Second lie, "She came to the police department about her son, and she wanted my advice on a situation she was having with him, and from there she would call me sometimes for advice."

I said, "First of all, bitch, you are not a counselor. You should have referred her to someone who could actually help her. There are plenty of resources available to parents, and second of all, she has your personal phone number, so you think I'm stupid?"

The next day, I called my niece. "Hey, I need for you to pull up at my house in the morning so I can load up all of Bobby's shit 'cause he's cheating, and he has to get the hell out of here."

When my niece arrived, we loaded up all his clothes in her car, then we loaded up his pickup truck with the rest of his clothes, military plaques, certificates, anything that had his name on it; we drove to his hometown; and I parked his truck in front of his brother's house; and we commenced to unload my niece's car and finished stuffing his truck with his belongings. His fat-ass brother came out of his house and sat on the porch, trying to tell me what his brother wasn't doing. I cussed his ass out, and I told him, "You don't know where he put his dick at, and mind your fucking business." I was hotter than a book of matches.

Don't fuck with a lady that's scorned. After Bobby's fellow officers heard about his unfortunate departure from the house, I learned that police officers will defend the code of duty and the code of cheating. It's not okay. The concern for his well-being was mind-boggling. Cause why are you guys coming to my house? To get me to let him come back home? This one officer really went overboard and said, "You should let Bobby come home because he really looks bad." I was thinking, *He has been gone for two weeks, and you think he looks bad?* but I said, "Okay, I'll take that into consideration." I don't know if Bobby went to our pastor or if someone else told our pastor but one day, to my surprise, our pastor showed up at our house, and he wanted to talk to me about my marriage. My pastor knew I admired him and valued his opinion, so I actually listened to him, and I decided to let him come back home, but I wish I would have stuck to my instincts and just let the marriage dissolved into a divorce.

Don't let other people guide your decisions. You got to live for you, and your happiness is all that really matters. Throughout this marriage, I came to find out that my husband listened to his friends, his family about how to live his life, even how to treat my kids. He didn't want my children to call him daddy; he told my children to just call him Bobby right in front of his brothers that were visiting us—so that's how you are going to be a big man in front of your family, and they all laughed. It wasn't funny to me, but you are going to get your wish. They are going to call you by your name because they've got a father. Anytime I wanted to improve the quality of life for us together, he didn't want to do it; he always looked to the negative side of everything since I didn't need his approval to accomplish a task. I am a strong, successful, independent, stubborn, determined, ambitious woman, and I didn't need to ask for his financial support. I'm trying to manage my home and my business. I have moved once again in a larger facility because God is in the blessing business, and he is truly blessing me.

Although the day care seems like a blessing and a curse, I knew it was what God wanted me to do—it was my calling—but it was really becoming stressful. The day care had taken a toll on me. No one knew all the sleepless nights, all the nights that I stayed up crying. If something happened at the center, how I would wonder how I'm going to get out of this mess. How am I going to pay this parent who was looking for some money?

I started to take sleeping pills. I started to take anxiety pills. I started taking pills for depression. I had been on these pills for years without anyone even knowing it except for immediate family and close workers. No one knows when you have paid a light bill for a parent or helped a family purchase a car or took food to a family in need. I have done all of that and didn't give it a second thought because I'm chosen to do God's will; whether it was appreciated or not wasn't my concern. I'm making sure that these kids are taken care of. Budgeting and having common sense are all it really takes to operate a day care center, making sure that you stay on top of your game when it comes to your business.

I'm going to the food bank. I'm on the food program, paying all my bills, making sure my workers are getting paid, and making sure that my local, state, and federal taxes are paid. The day care center always brought me heartache and pain; it was always something. We were being accused of my staff not being trained properly; we were trained by the state training facilities. We had our hours that we needed to keep teaching. Certifications were always up-to-date. We had regular staff meetings. We did everything by the book. Every year we would keep up with the standard guidelines that was required. Yes, any day care will have minor deficiencies that we would have to fix. Overall, I had a damn good center. We fed the kids home-style meals. People in the streets said we didn't feed the children, that their children always came home hungry, but they sure left them there after their hours, so they would get fed or take plates home.

When people see you growing, they try to figure out a way to stop you. They first start to scandalize your name because that's the deadliest way to kill someone's character, then they use the Internet, social media, which is the fastest way to flat out spread lies—either way, you are doomed. Everyone doesn't believe what they hear or read, but 85 percent of the people do. It's like you are fighting a losing battle before the fight begins. Luckily, I have always been a praying woman. Once I found God, I decided that I wasn't going to let him go. I knew that Jesus was my only help and hope that existed in my life. At the end of the day, I had no one that I could depend on, no one that understood what I was going through, and no one that understood this pain that I felt inside.

Kanisha was one of my loyal workers. She worked for me for about eighteen years until I closed my business. We were like sisters. I trained her to be my director, and she knew what I liked and what I didn't like. She operated my day care center like I did, so I didn't worry when she was there. Kanisha was the boss on the first shift, and I enjoyed going in the afternoon because that was the time I was needed the most. The time children came from school was the most chaotic time of the day and the busiest. If anything occurred, I would be there to directly deal with any situation.

No matter how many training classes your teachers attend, human error is eventually going to happen. I could not satisfy every parent when accidents occurred, whether it was serious or not. My reputation as a business owner took a hit, and I had to handle things the best way I knew how because this was my passion, and sometimes in life, we must take the good with the bad. But I always felt like we as day care workers were often unappreciated, overworked, and underpaid. When DHR changed the child ratio, it made things harder for the small business owners like myself. On top of all my problems now, I must hire two teachers for every classroom, adding to the fact that I had more money going out than I had coming in. Budgeting was my strong suit. I made struggling look convincing. To keep the morale up at the day care, I gave my workers Christmas parties and bonuses and celebrated Teacher Appreciation Day each year. I wanted them to know that I cared about them as employees and gave thanks to God for allowing me to continue to take care of his little children. My staff keeps me motivated. We had some good times. We joked around, laughed, and talked smack to one another.

It was just like being at a family get-together. I had a closer relationship with my staff than I did with my own family.

Everything was running smoothly until the owner of the building decided to sell the building that I worked on to make it a day care. I purchased everything that was put into the building. When I didn't meet his deadline for me to purchase the building, he didn't consider anything that I had done to the building—all he was interested in was making money. I had gone to several banks, trying to purchase the building. It didn't matter to the bank how many years I had been in business; it didn't matter how good my credit score was. They would have me thinking that they were going to finalize the loan up until the last day of me waiting for an approval and call to tell me the deal didn't go through. I would always be devastated because I was really trying to purchase this building. I had spent a lot of money to make this mine. It seemed as if I couldn't win for losing, gathering up all that information that they requested, getting a budget prepared by a professional. It is heartbreaking how they can set you up for a letdown.

Now, I was out searching for a new building. I had a friend that would help me with tax papers. She informed me of a building across town. I wasn't really interested because of the location; location is everything when it comes to day care. I never went to look at the facility until some of the owners of the building stopped by my business and asked me to come take a look at the building, so I decided to do so. This would be the worst decision of my professional life. Beware of wolves in sheep's clothing; they told me they would fix the building up to my liking, and I agreed to all of their demands because it was what I thought at the time in my best interest. I moved in the building. It was all the space that I had been looking for with a nice kitchen. It was perfect. My business hours were 4:30 a.m. to midnight. We accommodated the parents with three shifts. We had ten vans. God had truly blessed me. Oh, how my business flourished, and we had prospered because I always included my employees in my growth because without them and God, I couldn't have become so successful.

I appreciated God for choosing me to offer service to low-income families, providing transportation for a variety of services that was not required by the state. This was a personal decision. I enjoyed ministering to people and helping those less fortunate than myself. Often this big heart of mine has gotten me in trouble, and this service would not be exempt from accusations. My director and secretary always reminded me of being so vulnerable. We have a funny feeling about people's agenda, and hopefully, you are not allowing the same people to take advantage of you.

They say a hard head makes a soft ass. I wasn't listening to any of their advice because I felt my mission was all I needed to focus on. In the meantime, people are going to be rebellious against your rules. Some parents are great and provide their children with the necessities that they need and are important to them. But then you have those in the messy group, who seek validation from their friends and the street committee and are not going to comply with any of your rules or regulations. I'm guilty of allowing myself to be a part of that behavior. And when I decided that I had enough of some people not living up to their responsibilities as parents, I became the enemy, threating to stop the contumacy.

I couldn't understand why I was being tested time and time again. It was like I was suffering for being a good person. No way am I perfect; I'm not without sin. But my god! No matter how I helped these people in this community, the worst things always came to me. I learned a valuable lesson about helping people: you're only hurting yourself. Even though I don't believe my work was in vain, I just think I helped the wrong people. I expected hate from strangers and associates, but from family? That's a different kind of hate. It was like everyone picked the family member that they were going to hang around. My nieces were messy sometimes. They were Carolyn's best friends, and sometimes they were my best friends. I stopped going to family functions because of the arguments that would take place. I didn't like the behavior, so I took myself and my children out of the equation. But you know, my family called it disowning them. How can you disown the bloodline you never chose? Now, if God would had given me a choice, I probably would have chosen a different family.

I often questioned my mother's love for me 'cause the lady just didn't show any emotions when it came to love. I wanted her to say, "I'm proud of you, baby!" for becoming a successful business owner. I wanted her to say, "Baby, do you need me to come help you at your day care sometimes?" She went faithfully every day to help my sister—just blatant disregard for my feelings.

I began to hear rumors regarding disrespectful conversations between my mother and my sister pertaining to me. I knew they were very capable of destroying a person's name. I believed that my mother's family was cursed with this behavior. My mother and her siblings didn't get along with one another. I couldn't understand why these people always talked about the past. They let whatever happened to them in their past destroy them as a family, and they watched their children do it to one another. When would this insanity stop? I wanted it to stop with my children and the younger generation. We all lived near family but didn't know their children nor grandchildren. You would think everyone lived hundreds of miles apart, but in reality, we probably only lived twenty to thirty minutes apart. That's crazy.

I taught my children to be close to one another. Of course, you will have disagreements, but you should always come together as a family when tempers have shimmered down and say, "I'm sorry." Someone must be the bigger person 'cause tomorrow is not promised to anyone. If you lose a loved one, that's when people have regrets. That's when it's too late to turn back the hands of time.

We could have been a family like we were in the old days before money got involved in our lives and became an issue, but instead, we let the twenty years of us being in business destroy our relationship. Neither one of us knew that one day these day cares we own would ruin both of our lives. My family had become my worst nightmare, and me being the youngest of seven children, they felt as if Carolyn should be more successful than me. That became a controversy within the family.

Carolyn wanted to control everyone's lives, and I wasn't going for it. I am my own person. We both are ladies who should be able to control our own lives and make our own decisions. I didn't need her to fight my battles anymore; I was very capable of solving my own problems. When my nephew went to prison, he was sentenced to twenty years. No one thought that he would get released early because he had federal time. Everyone felt bad for him, and we wanted to do something to help him, but there wasn't anything anyone could do. I personally don't think he was represented by a good attorney, but he chose who he wanted.

My nephews didn't act like the women in our family. They would say that everyone needs to try to stick together and be a family. I didn't see them as often as I would have liked, but they are men. We shouldn't expect men to hang around a bunch of women gossiping. I went to his sentencing day in Montgomery at the courthouse. They had him all shackled up like he had killed somebody. He is a small-size man. I almost started crying when I had to sit there and listen to this judge tell him, "I hereby sentence you to twenty years in the federal pen." That does something to the soul to hear that, and you know you are powerless. He would often call, and I would be glad to hear his voice.

On one of the calls he made to me, he said, "Cynt, will you handle some of my business that I didn't get a chance to?"

I said, "What do you need for me to do?"

He said, "Try to save my house. You can keep my Tahoe, and I need for you to put my money up for me. You are going to need to have power of attorney over all my possessions because I trust you, and I know you will take care of my belongings."

I said, "You know you can trust me, and I promise I won't give anyone anything unless you tell me to."

So I accepted his request, and I also said, "You know, everybody is going to be mad because you didn't choose them."

He said, "I don't care who gets mad because I want to have something left so when I do get out. I can restart my life."

When everybody found out he left me in control, the rumors started. Everyone was pissed off, and it only was because they thought he had a million dollars, and he didn't, so I just let them talk like the fools that they are. One day I was at the day care center, and I got a phone call from Bobby.

He said, "Cynt, get up here to the house quick. Come on now, don't wait. Stop whatever you are doing and come now."

I said, "What's going on?"

He said, "Just do what I asked you. Your mother, Carolyn, and Annie are up here to the house demanding to get all of Chico's belongings, and when you get here, give them everything of his."

I told Bobby, "I'm not giving them shit."

I left the day care, and I drove home. When I pulled up in my driveway, sure enough, all three of them were sitting in the car, and they all looked mad. It was momma bear, baby bear, and boss bear. Carolyn was sitting in the car under the steering wheel. When I got out of my car, my mother and my sister Annie got out the car, and nobody spoke to me.

I said to myself, "Oh, hell, there's some shit stirring in the air."

When we got in my kitchen, I said, "Momma, what's going on?"

She asked, "Did you pay Chico's attorney?"

I said, "Yes, I did. I called and told you that, plus I have the receipt from the bank that he told me to deposit the money in."

She said, "Well, we need you to give us all his stuff."

My sister was standing there, all swollen like a balloon as if she was going to burst at any moment. So finally, my sister erupted. "I guess my mother wasn't telling me off." Good enough for her. She started saying, "We want all his shit and his money too. I don't know why he left everything with you because he didn't even come up here to see you."

I said, "What the hell has that got to do with any of this? You are not getting shit because he didn't tell me to give any one of you his stuff, and you are not getting it. You're right—don't none of you all come to see me, and I don't give a fuck."

When I was walking toward my sister, Bobby knew this was getting ready to be a fight. He got between us, and he said, "Annie, leave now. Leave our home now. Y'all didn't have to come up here with that bull crap. Leave here now. I mean it, Annie, just go."

She acted as if she was hesitant to go, but if she wouldn't have hurried up and gotten out of our house, I was going to commence whopping on that ass. She was going to beat me, or I was going to beat her. I knew Carolyn was the instigator behind that whole incident that occurred at my house that day, that's why she didn't get out the car. She let them handle her dirty work for her. I was so hurt when they left because finally someone admitted to my face that the family doesn't give a fuck about me. What have I done to make these people hate me so much? Why does being ambitious cause people to despise you just because I'm independent and I don't have to beg anyone in my family to help. I think they would have been happy if I would have stayed in that abusive relationship and didn't aspire to be anyone or have anything, but that wasn't me. I am everything that an entrepreneur sets out to be and become successful beyond your imagination, but I'm thinking, *Lady, you birthed me. Didn't you once love that little girl you brought home from the hospital and watch her grow into a successful woman? Why would you make differences between the children that you carried for nine months? Why are you involved in this drama that your children have going on, that your daughters have going on against another one of your children? Why don't you love me? What is your problem, woman? Why do you hate me so much? I didn't ask to be born in this world—you brought me here—so why are you treating me like this?*

A mother's love means a lot to all of us, but when you don't have that love from your mother, that is a different hurt, a different pain. I have been mistreated all my life by somebody, and I'm the type of person that will do anything for anyone, and all I ever wanted was to be loved by my mother. I continued to hold on to as much of my nephew's belongings that I could. I couldn't keep his house because I couldn't make two mortgage payments—his and mine. I built a storage house on my property, and I put all his furniture inside the storage unit. I kept my promise. I put his money up in a safe place for him, and no one else came to take stake in his belongings.

As a surprise to us all, when President Obama got ready to leave office from his second term, Chico received a pardon from the president, and he was released after serving eight years. It was truly a blessing from above, and he is now an entrepreneur. Anyone can change their life if they are given a chance. Serenity: home is where the heart is. I am a very laid-back individual, so every Saturday morning, I would get up and clean my entire house. After that, I would go on my back porch, sit in my favorite chair, and listen to music. I wasn't partying anymore. I didn't like to go out to movies. I didn't really like to go out to eat. All I like to do on the weekend was just sit on that back porch and rock my world away unless I went fishing, which I enjoyed. I didn't have a lot of friends that I hung out with. My employees were really the only family that I had since my family didn't really visit me.

My children would often say, "Mama, won't you go out to eat or go to the movies?"

I would reply, "I'm fine back here."

I was living my life on my back porch. They would even invite me to go out with them, and I would say no. One of my daughters was like, "Mama? Let's start going on vacations like everybody else does. All these people go on vacations every year, and we just sit here at the house and do nothing."

I started thinking, *You make enough money to go on vacation. Even your employees go on vacations, and you're the owner. Why are you not taking your family on vacations?*

It made sense, but I still wasn't quite ready. So operating my business and enjoying my home was my life when my son was attending military school back in my small hometown, his last two years of school. He was getting in trouble big time, getting expelled from the school, being accused of using drugs. This boy was about to give me a heart attack. He knew how upset he was making me. He knew the only thing I asked of all three of my kids is "Bring home your high school diploma, and hopefully, you will go to college."

One time when he was in trouble, he wrote me this heartfelt letter. I cried when I read that letter. It touched my heart, and then he wrote me a song. When I talked to him on the phone, he sung that song to me. I really thought that my son was trying to make a change for the better and that he was really going to graduate. When I was called in the office about his behavior among other things and the possibility of him not getting a chance to graduate, I was broken.

I expressed my concern to the general, and I told him, "Please give him another chance because he deserves the opportunity to receive his high school diploma." I promised the general that I would stay on Trevon regarding his homework and the importance of his education and that his playtime was over. While he was at the military academy, he learned from his instructor that a young man from Opelika had been murdered in the projects, and he learned that this was his cousin / best friend. He was devastated to know that Jamal had been killed. He called me crying, asking me if it was true about Jamal. I hesitated because I didn't know how to tell a seventeen-year-old boy that yes, your best friend is dead.

He told me, "Mama, I feel so lost. A part of me died when Jamal left this world because he was my best friend, and he taught me about the streets. He told me how to handle myself in the street and how he didn't want me to get in trouble like he was getting in trouble, and he always told me, 'Trevon, make sure you become someone in life.'"

He told me that Jamal inspired him to sing, and I am glad that Jamal made a positive impact on my son's life. Trevon received his high school diploma. I was so proud of him. He later started college at the Art Institute in Atlanta after his cousin Brandon had enrolled. Trevon courses included music, video and other instrumental classes.

As any young adult who was in college, free to spend Momma and Daddy's money and don't have a care in the world, they always find the wrong crowd and start skipping classes, but he always needed money for school. I wasn't thinking that he was up to his usual stunts; I was thinking he was in college—everything was good. I was purchasing food. I didn't want my son going around Atlanta hungry, plus he had his vehicle, so he could come home on the weekends as often as he likes. Why my son found the bad crowd of people to hang out with, I don't know.

He got pulled over by the police and must go to court, and here I was again, trying to convince the judge not to send him to jail for a year.

When it was his turn to go before the judge, the judge asked him, "Son, do you smoke marijuana?"

My son said, "No, Your Honor. I don't smoke marijuana."

The judge told him, "Have a seat, son, and think about what you just told me. And when I call you back up here, make sure you give me the right answer. If not, I'm going to give you a year in jail."

I went and I sat down next to my son, and I told him, "If you don't tell this judge the truth that you smoke marijuana, your ass is going to be in jail for a year. So I suggest that you tell the truth when he calls you back up there."

When the judge called his name to come back before him and the judge said, "Son, are you ready to tell me the truth?" my son said, "Yes, sir."

"Do you smoke marijuana?"

He said, "Yes, sir."

The judge informed, "My son, if it wasn't for your mother and you telling the truth this time, you were facing a year in jail."

My son said, "Thank you, Your Honor."

The judge said, "You are free to go home."

I told Trevon to stop riding with these guys and smoking marijuana. "You don't know anything about these people."

I had no idea that he had dropped out of school. I was still sending him money like he asked. I was still traveling to Atlanta to purchase food. He didn't tell me anything. I was thinking after this incident with the police, he was going to go to class and walk the straight and narrow road until one weekend I was in Atlanta to visit my son. He had walked out to go to the store. My nephew Brandon was his roommate.

He said, "Aunt Cynt, you do know that Trevon isn't in school anymore." He had not told me that he was not enrolled in school anymore, so Brandon said, "Let him tell you because I don't want him to get mad at me."

I said, "Don't worry. I'm going to act like I don't know a thing."

That was how I found out that my son was not enrolled at the college anymore. I think I let him play that college game on me for about two more weeks before I busted him with "The gig is up. I know you're not in college anymore, so bring your ass home."

I made him come back home and look for a job. He showed a lot of interest in the day care, so I hired him as a van driver. He told me that one day he wanted to operate my center. For me, he seemed to enjoy it. Despite all of the challenges we faced daily, it definitely was a bad time for one of the members on the committee who rented the building to me to pass away. His death affected everything because he made promises that the other members have now voided out. I knew everything was going to go downhill from there, and it did. I started to have problems with them. They didn't want to honor the wishes of the person who passed. He was truly a good man, and he told me he wanted me to purchase that building; but when the head dies, the tail just wiggles away, and that's when you are in trouble.

They were pressuring me to purchase the building and went up on the price. No matter how hard I tried to get a loan to purchase this building from the bank, my credit was never good enough. I never had enough assets. The bank never saw fit for me to pay them back. If I'm paying my rent, why can't I pay you?

It is designed for failure against the people of color. I don't have anything against different races of people—some of my best friends are White—but I do know that every White person that goes into a bank is not qualified for a loan, but they get approved because of their skin color. All these buildings in America are owned by the corporate world of White America. Why bring us here if we can't benefit from the same standards set up for you? We as Black people will never be able to experience some of the things that our white brothers and sisters have accomplished. When you first walk through the bank doors and you ask for an application for a loan, your color has determined the status of your application—you have already been denied. If you are lucky enough to get approved, I bet you your last dollar you got some White friends that know people in the right places. The game is definitely not fair. So I was stuck, didn't know which way to turn. I couldn't commit to the price of this building—it was not worth the price that they were asking for. I had spent my own money helping to make this building the dream that I had, that I envisioned, and it was looking amazing, but Black people will let greed stop their growth every time.

You name it, it happened in that building. It's like I had gone to hell and came straight back, and I couldn't see my way out. When I tell you everything was happening in that building, I'm not lying. Everyone was out to get me. My depression, anxiety, and insomnia were at an all-time high. Looked like when we would solve one problem, here came another; and to top that off, my sister Carolyn would call me on the phone, asked me if a particular parent enrolled her kids in my day care center. Of course, I was going to say no to her because either way, she would cuss me out and say don't enroll any more of her damn parents. I would fuss back with her and let her know these people can take their kids to any day care they want to, and I was open for business. She would be too hot at me. When a parent or someone from the streets would come to my day care to fight one of us, they were going to have to fight the whole crew—that's how we stuck together. People thought because I was so sweet and carried myself in a professional way, that I didn't have any hood in me.

This young lady had been pressuring me to hire her, and I wasn't going to hire her because of her reputation in the streets; so one day, she came to the day care and embarrassed me in front of some of my teachers and the kids. I kept my composure. I let her speak her mind, and I didn't say a word, so she thought I was afraid of her, but she didn't know she was messing with a sleeping lion. So a couple of days later, I had got to the day care early that morning, about 7:30 a.m. or 8:00 a.m. Myself, my director, and my cook were sitting in the office. I was on the computer, placing a food order from a local grocery store. This girl entered my office and started fussing and cussing at me about not hiring her.

You want to talk about my blood boiling and going into overdrive. I took my fist, pounded down on my computer desk so hard, looked her in her eyes, and told her if she didn't get the hell out my office, "I'm going to beat your ass."

She looked at me as though she was shocked and turned around and ran out my office so fast I never had to worry about her again. Don't let this size and pretty face fool you, boo, but through all the controversies, I and my employees manage to pick up the pieces and have a good time, and I continued to show them my appreciation through parties. My staff was my family. We would have some of the best times at the day care center. Two of my employees, Sarah and Tania, had been working for me for over twenty years; Kanisha, my director, eighteen years; and Derrick for fifteen years and on down. I had some loyal people, and you always look out for those type of people. My employees had great relationships with one another. They always kept me laughing because they were always up to some foolishness. When you spent every day with good people, it's hard to let them go.

I prayed to God, "Take this business away from me. Give me something else to do in my life. I can't take this anymore. What is it going to take for me to get out of this, to get some relief, to be stress-free?" I prayed daily, and I worshipped daily for God to give me a new life, a new beginning, a fresh start, and they always say, "Be careful what you wish for—your wishes might come true."

Yes, my director and a couple more of my employees always tried to comfort me and tell me that we were going to be okay, don't worry, but the only person that could really hear my cries is Jesus, and only Jesus could save me. Without him in my life, I don't think I could have made it the times that I did. I haven't always had good employees; I have had some bad ones as well. They would sit back and call DHR on you and come to work as if they haven't done a thing. They have reported me to the food bank and got me disqualified from participating in the program. I even had a mother and a daughter that I had known for years sit in on a meeting to have my day care closed because they were related to a parent whose child was supposed to have been in an incident at the day care center. I couldn't believe these people would do that especially after I helped her daughter keep her job with me, and she was still able to work with children because she was accused of beating a child at my center, and I saved her from that situation. The cousin of the mother and daughter that had worked for me went around town, telling everyone that she was going to be the one to shut my doors down and that she was going to sue me and that she would be the owner of my day cares, plus she was going to rename the centers. You definitely put your hands in shutting me down, but don't count your chickens before your eggs hatch; you're not entrepreneurship material because the God I serve will place his wrath upon you all. Don't mess with God's chosen people.

I wish I would have let DHR have their way with her because she and her momma aren't any good, they are lowdown people, and I have had employees plot up to quit working for me at the same time. I had it happen twice—once at Tiny Tots, and the second time was at Jumpstart day care. On the second time it happened, my mother had passed, and two sisters that were working for me quit when my mother was being buried. There are some coldhearted people in this world, but God still covered me. I have had employees stealing time; stealing from the kitchen pots pans, utensils, and even food; but not my Tania. She didn't steal. Employees going out scandalizing my name, and they didn't work there anymore, just not appreciating me as a boss and a person. I have had incidents to occur like a child being left in the day care center after hours. I had to pay that parent so she wouldn't tell on me. Also being accused of a child being left on the van—it was good that, that allegation was unfounded—and being accused of children being left on the playground. What I couldn't understand was how a child can get hurt on the playground while in a teacher's care and also the classroom if you are doing your job.

My day care was now being put on the famous Facebook. It was enough to drive any sane person to insanity. My medication was not working. My doctor was increasing the doses. Even while taking sleeping pills, I would not be able to sleep. I could go without days of sleep. When I mentioned what I was experiencing with my doctor, he sent me to a specialist, and he recommended a sleep apnea test which came out negative. I had been going through all kinds of emotional highs and lows until one night, I had to go to the emergency room, and I was prescribed Ambien.

I was thinking, *Lord, what am I going to do?*

As life continued and my day care world was still a roller-coaster ride, then I developed pneumonia and had to be put in the hospital for five days. I was thinking that my husband would have my back. One day, when he came to see me at the hospital, I could tell that he had something on his mind. So before he got ready to leave, he told me that he was going to ride with his nephew to Montgomery.

I said, "For what?" while I'm in this hospital; I was so pissed off. "You have only been here a couple of hours, and I'm sick. I need you by my side. You should have been saying, 'I'm going home to get some clothes so I can come back and spend the night with you.' But instead, you want to ride out of town with your nephew. Well, ain't that a bitch? So if you choose to go to Montgomery instead of staying here with me, have all your shit packed and ready to go when I get home."

We had an argument at the hospital. I wouldn't be thinking about going out of town if he was in the hospital—that let you know when a person is not committed to their marriage. I was tired of having to be put on the calendar. When I needed him to fix a toilet at the day care, I must be put on a calendar. When I needed him to do chores around the house, every time I asked this man to do anything, he put me on his damn calendar.

"Who are you? I thought I was the business owner, but never mind me, maybe you're the business owner."

It was beyond me how I didn't realize that he did not take this marriage seriously. When he brought me home from the hospital and got me settled in, it was early one morning.

He asked me, "Do you want me to go out and get you some breakfast?"

I thought that was so thoughtful of him. I said yes. "Can you go to Tyler's and bring me a breakfast back?"

This man left here to go get breakfast. After he was gone for an hour, I said to myself, "Where did he go to get breakfast?" I wanted to give him the benefit of the doubt without accusing him of doing something, but another thirty minutes passed, so I decided to call his phone. He never answered the phone. It rang back to back to back. At this point, I was angry. It doesn't take an hour to pick up breakfast, and he was not answering his phone. It took him two hours to get back with the breakfast that only should have taken at least twenty minutes or twenty-five minutes at the most to bring back home.

If he wasn't cheating, I don't know what to call it. His excuse for not answering the phone for me was he was on the phone with a guy that he worked with on the police department. "So you're telling me you didn't answer the phone because you are on the phone with a guy. You must think I'm a fool. Oh, I'm going to find out what's going on, and when I do, your ass is going to be in trouble."

One thing about people, they are going to find the time to cheat no matter what it does to the marriage or what the spouse brings to the table. Being faithful is a difficult task and a hard commitment to uphold. The old folks say it's a fifty-fifty commitment in a marriage or relationship, but I swear mine was an eighty-twenty in my favor. Everybody doesn't have your best interest at heart. Sometimes you are sleeping with the enemy. Anytime you must beg your partner to help you or convince them that the choices you are making is for the family and they try to undermine every move you make, they are not for you. We can disagree there isn't anything wrong with that. Everyone is entitled to their own opinion and have their own beliefs, but not meeting me halfway on anything until the product is finished doesn't sit well with me. Now once again, I was not in a happy marriage. I was not getting abused, but my marriage was unevenly yoked. We didn't have the same views. We didn't have the same values. We didn't want the same things. I am hungry for success. I like new business ventures. I'm not afraid when it comes to starting a new business. I listened to my husband's nephew and went out and purchased an eighteen-wheeler truck—a business I knew nothing about but through him being a truck driver.

In saying that he would drive for us, I took him up on the idea of purchasing this truck. Once I purchased the truck, he drove for a little while, and the truck broke down a couple of times, and I had to get it fixed. I found out that this was an expensive repair that I wasn't ready for. Of course, I had credit cards, and this was how I managed to pay for the repairs. I would pay him even though I wasn't making any money off the truck, and I would let him borrow money that he wouldn't even pay back. But then he decided to stop driving the truck because he said, "I'm not going to make you all rich."

"What do you mean make us rich? This purchase has damn near broken me financially."

I wanted to cuss his ass out so bad I didn't know what to do, so I decided to let my husband handle it "'Cause that's your stupid-ass nephew."

What's wrong with Black people? If you can drive for a White person, you can drive for me. This was your idea—to purchase this truck. You came to our house every day, buttering me up, talking me into this. You made it sound like sugar and spice and everything nice."

I'm here to tell you your family will fuck you up every time. They make all these promises that they're not going to keep. I held up my end of the bargain. I purchased this big truck that I didn't even need. Now this was another situation that I was placed where my money just went down the drain. Now who was I going to find to drive this truck?

I had one guy that was working out perfectly but encountered so many breakdowns that after paying him; I was still losing out. It was just a disaster, another financial setback, so I tried to sell the truck, and I wasn't having any luck until my cousin Vincent told me about this guy that he knows who was looking to purchase a truck. When I tell you beware of scammers, I mean just that. This guy and his wife came to our house like they were legit people. They came with all the proper paperwork. I didn't have to do anything but read over the documents and sign because he was going to make monthly installments to me, so he wouldn't be able to transfer the title in his name until the final payment was made.

Like I said, beware of scammers. This guy made one payment to me on my truck, and I never heard from him again until one day the truck broke down in Atlanta, and he called my husband, talking about when we were going to come and get the truck. First off, no, you aren't making any payments to me on this eighteen-wheeler rig, and you are expecting us to come all the way to Atlanta to pick up a truck that you are using to make money from? No, sir, I'm not going to do it.

So after he found out I wasn't a big dummy that he thought I was, he had to get the truck from Atlanta himself. I didn't hear from him again. I went and hired an attorney to try to get my truck from this guy. The attorney sent him several certified letters. He never responded back. After numerous attempts to contact this dude to no avail, it was costing me money for the attorney to continue this case, so I dropped it, and I said God will handle it like he always does.

Years later, he called me out of the clear blue sky and threatened me about a truck that he clearly has taken, and I quote, "I'm going to bring your truck—oh, it's my truck now—to your house and dump it in your yard."

Bitch, the devil is a liar. "Why do you think you are going to bring me a truck that doesn't work anymore? No, I don't want it— you keep it. It's benefiting you more than it is benefiting me. But threatening me, bitch, I'm like the state of Missouri. Show me 'cause if you come on this private property, you better bring the law 'cause it's going down."

Yes, I lost a lot of money in this transaction, but baby, the headache that I had from that truck—believe me, I don't want it anymore, and I am truly unbothered, and they didn't show up—all talk and no action. There I go having this big-ass heart wanting to help everybody. I was slowly learning that you can't help everybody. Every time somebody needed a car, I was there to help them with the down payment. Every time someone needed cash, I was there to loan money to them; and majority of the time, I wouldn't even get it back. I'm here helping family members who don't even care about me, helping my niece move from house to house, even helping her furnish her place because I knew she needed my help, and I didn't like to see people suffer when I can clearly be of assistance. I was always somewhere lending a helping hand to someone else; I feel like God has blessed me, and he wants me to be a blessing to others.

But at the same time, I was only hurting myself. The outside world didn't know the struggle that I was going through. They didn't know the pain that I was suffering through. Through it all I kept a smile on my face. No one knew that inside, I was dying. I was dying because I was in financial trouble. I was robbing Peter to pay Paul. I was borrowing money from four payday loan companies to pay my employees, sometimes to buy groceries, to pay the light bill, the water bill.

I stayed strong. I was determined to make it. I would do anything to keep my business going—that was my life. People didn't realize I didn't have the support from my husband that I needed and yearned for, to be the woman and the man in the relationship and having the highest income in the house. When you don't have a partner who can come close to or match your income, jealousy and envy sets in, and they become a burden because when you need help, they can't help you. When you ask for help, they don't want to help you. No, he wasn't abusing me, but I was still suffering physical stress, psychological stress, and psychospiritual stress. It was the will of God that I survived. Not only do I have the day care business, I have a mobile home business where I go out and I purchase mobile homes and I remodel them. So I'm the one who must pick out everything that I need for this mobile home, and I have to pay for everything. Luckily, I have had a gentleman that has worked for me over ten years remodeling my homes. Even though we argued about every little thing when it comes to remodeling, when he's finished, it is an awesome home that anyone would love to live in.

I keep my properties up-to-date. When something breaks down, my tenants know that I'm coming—just give me a little time, but I'm going to get it fixed for you. Everyone knows that I'm about my business. I don't like playing around when it comes to people's livelihood. I'm a one-stop-shop person, and I truly believe that's why God continues to bless me. Even in my worst days, he still blesses me.

Maybe family won't be so bad. I was hiring everyone else, so I decided to hire three of my nieces, and I would let my brother come in and help me sometimes. My brother wasn't the type of person that you really would want to work for you because he felt entitled to your business because I'm his sister. No, you're not entitled to my business. You cannot fire my staff just because they won't sleep with you. You cannot fire my staff just because they won't do what you ask them to do. You are not their boss—I am their boss.

When I wasn't at work, my brother would walk around that building like he owned it. He would go to all the classrooms and tell those teachers how to do their jobs and what they're doing wrong and what they need to do. He has not had one course on certification to be a teacher. So why? He was trying to handle my business. These teachers have been properly trained and are certified to work in the day care field. When they wouldn't respond to his demands, he would tell them, "You're fired," or, "I'm going to tell my sister to fire you."

I kept telling him, "You cannot do that. If you keep going to my teachers' classes and threatening their jobs, I am going to let you go." I don't think he took me seriously—not one time.

I tried to give my brother the benefit of the doubt by saying, you know, he grew up with all these sisters, so of course, he's going to be messy, and my mother babied him, when I was actually the baby, but I swear I couldn't tell. She always took up for him, and everything that he did, my mother didn't see any wrong in my brother; everything he told her when he went home, she would believe him—every word that came out of his mouth—and someone in the streets always started an argument with him. It was never his fault. We knew better, but you couldn't tell that to our mother—I guess she loved her son.

There wasn't any excuse for the way he behaved, and I wasn't going to put up with the behavior that she allowed herself to put up with. "I'm your sister, not your mother, and I'm going to tell you when you are wrong."

When he would get mad with you, he would retaliate against you. He would spread lies in the community about you. He would call my husband and tell him that I was cheating with guys whom I employed on my job. I'm more professional than that. He would do anything to hurt you just because he believes in payback, and this is not how you pay a person back that's trying to help you. I had tried to help him establish his own business—that didn't work for him either.

What does surprise me is when you go to our uncle's house to try to recruit some crackheads to come to my business and break my windows at the day care. That was beyond my comprehension. Does it matter to you that we grew up together? Does it matter to you that we struggle together? Our mother wasn't rich, but she said that if you want something, work for it. Don't take anything that doesn't belong to you. Go out and make something out of yourself—and that's what I did. You had the same opportunity to do what I did. You really were the first business owner in the family. You started your own carpet cleaning business. I wish it would have worked out for you. I don't know what you did to lose it, but believe me, I really wish it would have worked out for you. Maybe you wouldn't be so envious of your sisters. Maybe I could call you my brother because for the evil you have done to me, you are truly dead to me. This is a relationship that will never be rekindled, and I put Mary had a little lamb on that?

When you don't do right by people, everything you touch will fail. When you have an evil heart, God cannot bless you through that mess that you have inside you.

I decided I have given you too many chances, but I know what I'm not going to do is continue to have you in my life, and I can't trust you. I decided from then on that my cousin Vince would be the one to help me at the day care. Plus, Vince was a good-hearted person. He had good intentions, and he enjoyed working outside. He thought he could perform any task that was set before him. When we were in the club life, Vince would often be one of the security guards at the door. You couldn't tell him anything. He had his badge and handcuffs on his side and his flashlight. He thought he was a policeman back then.

When I hired him to work for me at the day care center, this man brought his handcuffs, his security badge, and always still carry a flashlight. I don't think he understood he would come in and work with kids. I guess he thought he would be coming to lock somebody up, and he always carried this notebook around that had thirty-year-old pictures of girls that he used to date or he was just friends with. This man brought this stuff to work every day. Then he found a spot in the day care to keep all his personal items—it was so funny to us.

My cousin helped me out a lot at the day care. I didn't have to wait on my husband anymore to complete a task that I needed done. I didn't have to call someone and pay them unnecessary money for something that we could actually fix ourselves. He would unload the van after we went out and got the groceries. He would keep the bathroom clean until I decided to hire a janitor. He was mainly hired for traffic control because the day care center was large, and we had three hundred kids enrolled. When the parents would come and pick up their kids, it would be congested out in the parking area, so we had to make sure that people were coming right out of the center, get in their car and leave, and not have traffic back up in the streets, which happened often. The day care center was not located in the safest area of town, so we would have to make sure first that all the children were off the van once the van drivers had completed their day. The secretary had to check behind the van driver to ensure that no children were left inside the van.

Once that was done, the drivers locked the doors to the vans so no one could steal the battery, radio, nor the van through the night. The parents were given codes to the entrance door of the building, and we checked the IDs of every person that was unknown to us when they were picking up children. Even though I had cameras inside and outside of the building, that didn't deter thieves that roamed the neighborhood. One morning, when Vincent arrived at work, he was checking the vans as usual. He checked all the fluid levels, and upon checking the tires for low tire pressure, he noticed that one of the tires had some lugs missing. He informed the director, and they both went outside to confirm what he found.

My director called me on the phone to inform me of the loose tire lugs. Not only did that phone call remind me of when my van was burned to the ground at my other day care center years ago, but it also reminded me that I still have an enemy out here in this world who will go to any lengths to destroy me. Either this person or persons hate my guts and the person who I have evolved into, or they have allowed jealousy to take control of their life from the accomplishments in my life that God has given me. If this van would have been driven with these children inside this van, there would have been an accident. That would have put my day care at risk, my livelihood at risk, parents' confidence in relying on us to get their kids back and forth to school in a safe fashion, and it could have caused me to close at that time.

This all goes to show you how far a person will go to destroy everything that you have built, what people will do to stop what God has given you. Yes, I have enemies, and they are lined up like crabs in a bucket. Who can get to the top first? Who will be the one to put the nail in the coffin? It won't be long before everyone finds out who are the devil's activists. I promise you my cousin Vincent was always ready to do whatever I asked of him. This particular day we went and rented a backhoe, he told me he knew how to operate this equipment.

This particular day, I needed some work done at the house, so we went, and we rented a small backhoe. He knew how to drive those big earthmoving equipment.

So when we get to the house, he was on top of this hill, and I had told him, "Vincent, don't go up there because it's dangerous."

"Oh, cousin, I can handle it."

Vincent was clearing the area around the shed, and I was cleaning my back porch. In my peripheral vision, I could see him losing control of the backhoe. I turned around, and I could see the machine turning over before it happened. I started screaming Vincent's name as loud as I could, then he hit the shed and was thrown off. At the same time, the backhoe burst into flames. Lord, I thought I was going to have a heart attack. I was so scared. When Vincent got up, he was limping.

I said, "Didn't I tell you to stay off that side of the shed 'cause it was too steep?"

Vincent said, "But, cousin, I had everything under control. I don't know what happened."

After I knew he was okay, of course, I cussed his ass out and told him, "I'm glad you didn't get hurt. Now stop doing shit you know you can't do."

I said, "I know what happened. Your ass almost got blown to pieces."

Oh, man, I thought I was going to have to pay for the equipment. Luckily, I got the insurance while I was there. Vincent was always pissing me off by tearing up stuff that he guaranteed me that he knew how to operate or how to do the job.

Vincent continued to come to the house to plant flowers for me, plant trees and cut the grass, take out the trash, or do anything that I needed done. On this day, my husband was picking at him about losing his girlfriend to his neighbor, and I had told him, "Bobby, stop messing with Vincent about that woman, he is getting upset. You're making him upset. He knows he lost his girlfriend to his neighbor. Stop bringing it up to him."

Bobby said, "I'm just joking around with him. I don't mean no harm, but he did lose her to the neighbor. Ha-ha-ha."

I said, "That's not funny, he really loved her; she just left him without an explanation, so of course, he is hurting. Love hurts. Just stop doing that to him. Don't mess with his feelings like that."

While Vincent was there driving my truck doing odd jobs, I went to the local hardware store to purchase some items that we needed. I was in line with a basket full of items. My phone began to ring. I answered my phone, and it was Bobby. He said, "Vincent has run over your Yorkie puppy."

I couldn't believe it. I asked him to repeat what he said.

"Vincent ran over your puppy, but it was an accident."

I was crying and saying, "Not my puppy! I know he didn't run over my puppy!"

Those people at the store was looking at me like this damn fool standing here, crying in line about a puppy. Yes, I was crying about my pet because I love my animals—I love all my pets.

When I got to the house, my little puppy was dead. Vincent kept saying, "I didn't see him, cousin, I'm sorry." I had a feeling that something was going to happen because Bobby kept taunting him about that girl, and Vincent was taking the breakup hard. Don't play with people's feelings especially when they're going through something. You'd never know how a person really feels inside about someone else, and everyone doesn't take breakups the same, but I still looked him in his eyes, and I told him, "You're going to pay me so

I can get another puppy," and I knew he didn't have seven hundred dollars to get me another Yorkie puppy. I told Vincent that I was going to take the money out of his check every week until he paid me, and guess what? I didn't take a dime out of his check. I just wanted him to feel my pain, so I just left it alone, and later I got me another puppy. Oh, Vincent—you couldn't live with him, and you couldn't live without him.

For the love of God, when the first of the month would roll around every month, I could not keep Vincent on the job. He would always stay out of work the first week of the month. No matter how many times I warned him repeatedly, he continued to do it. Finally, I was fed up with his shenanigans. He was taking a whole week off on the first of the month. We never had that agreement between us. The traffic wasn't stopping just because he took a week off work. I really needed him to control this traffic and to check those vans in the morning time. I started to feel like now he's taking advantage of me because we are family, and he's taking advantage of this job. If no other employees are getting away with staying out of work like that, why should I allow him to?

So one day, when he decided to return from his five-day vacation, he saw a new man in his position. He was mad at me for a long while, but eventually, he got over it, and he started going back to work at the trailers and at my house. As soon as he started back working on the trailers, he had an accident in my pickup truck, and it was a total loss, but he was still my buddy. When my daughter married in 2017, she had a beautiful wedding, and Vincent was doing his regular duties for me, helping with anything that I needed, but I did notice that Vince wasn't himself. He seemed to be tired, and he looked as if he was sick.

I went up to Vincent, and I asked him, "Are you okay?"

He replied, "I'm okay. I'm just a little hot."

I said, "Well, you need to stay out of this sun and stop overworking yourself. We got it from here."

But he wouldn't take no for an answer. He continued to help like he always would. Vincent and I were very close even though we would fuss and argue with one another. Vincent and I were inseparable. No matter what happened between our relationship, I was going to pick Vincent up because I knew that he was going to be the guy to help me with all my parties that I had for my staff, and he was always going to be the security man at the door like he was when we were younger, and he was not going to take any mess at the door. If you would start to act a fool at a party, he was going to escort you out, and he was going to always wear that security badge to let you know he was the police. There wasn't anyone else in the family I could count on other than Vincent.

I told Vincent that I would pick him up the following Tuesday, when I stopped by his house, I got sidetracked. I went in the house to speak to Aunt Doretha about some information I had gotten about my biological father, so I told Vincent that I would pick him up on Thursday. He said, "Cousin, whatever you got to do, we better go ahead and get it done and not to keep waiting around."

I said, "Okay," but he kept repeating it. I thought to myself, *Vincent just needs some money in his pocket*, and I went to work and got busy doing something else, and I didn't get a chance to pick him up that Thursday like I promised. I believe he had a premonition on him. From that Tuesday to that Thursday, everything kept getting in my way on my job, preventing me from going to pick Vincent up. When God has a plan, he doesn't let anyone get in the way. Always remember that. So I stopped by Aunt Doretha's house that Thursday evening on my way home to let Vincent know that I'm going to pick him up tomorrow morning, which was going to be Friday.

"Don't worry, I'll be here early in the morning, about eight o'clock. Be waiting for me."

"Okay," he said.

Okay, this all occurred two weeks after my daughter's wedding. Vincent's birthday was on August 22nd. My daughter married on August 5th. I was really going to pick him up this time. I was in my bed asleep, and my phone began to ring about 7:00 a.m. I do not like to get early morning phone calls because in my mind, they always consist of bad news, and bad news travels early in the morning. When I answered the phone, it was my Aunt Doretha.

She said, "Vincent has fallen out, and the ambulance is taking him to the hospital."

I said, "Oh my god, I'm on my way." I jumped out of bed as fast as I could. I put my clothes on as I was driving down the road, getting ready to turn on the hospital street. My phone rang again. It was Aunt Doretha.

She said, "You don't need to go to the hospital. Vincent has passed. He is gone."

I had to pull over on the side of the road. I was crying uncontrollably. I couldn't believe Vincent was gone. What was I going to do? I depended on him for so much. I took his death hard 'cause not only was he my cousin but also because he was my friend. We could talk about anything. I miss him to this very day. Rest in peace, cousin Vincent Heard.

Before my cousin Vincent died in 2017, I had another nephew, Petro. He was being released from prison, and he called to ask me could he come to stay at my house after being released from the halfway house. I have a two-story house; upstairs it has everything you need except a kitchen. Everyone wants to stay with me, and I have let a lot of people live upstairs—family members and nonfamily members. I am one of God's chosen people, so I must do his will, and a lot of times, I get in trouble for helping other people, but I always see the greater good in the assignment that I was given. Yes, sometimes I regret the decisions that I have made when helping someone else who is ungrateful, but that's not my concern. I pray about the situation, and God says, "Very well done, my child," and I know that he is happy with the obedience that I continue to show and do for his people—that's how I survive.

As my nephew continued to live with us, I was becoming increasingly unhappy in my marriage. I was tired of being the woman and the man. I was living a lie. The marriage didn't matter to me anymore. I couldn't tolerate the emptiness inside me. I didn't feel alive. I needed something more than being outdoors, watering my flowers, watching the birds feed from the birdhouse and the squirrels climbing the trees, listening to music, and sitting on the porch with the dogs and cats. They weren't fulfilling me anymore.

My nephew would hang around my son a lot, telling him about his life and letting him know that "you don't want to travel the road that I have been on," encouraging him to make plans and have goals set in life. My nephew wanted the easy life, which sometimes set you up for failure. Selling drugs is not the way unless you are willing to take the punishment that comes along with the crime. So throughout those conversations, my son did have goals and dreams that he wanted to accomplish. I did not know my son was writing music. I knew he wrote poetry as a kid, but I did not know he could sing because the little singing he did at that military school, you know it was okay, but he sounded like a beginner. I said, "That sounds good, son," because I didn't want to hurt his feelings. But the boy's voice had developed, and I didn't know it, and I guess my daughters and my future son-in-law and nephew were the only ones who knew that he had developed this talent.

One night I was upstairs cleaning out the closet for my nephew so that he could hang his clothes up and get all settled in. He came up to me one night, and he said, "You know you got a million dollars downstairs."

I replied, "What you mean I got a million dollars downstairs?"

He replied, "Your son Trevon can sing."

I laughed, and I said, "Trevon can't sing."

He said, "Yes, he can, Auntie. You haven't listened to him sing."

I said, "Not really."

I started taking items from upstairs to downstairs and throwing stuff in the trash. My son was standing by the kitchen sink, my daughter and her future husband were sitting on the kitchen stools, and music was playing. They all were bobbing their heads and smiling. I was thinking, *Just look at them. They all are high on marijuana.*

I was looking at my son. He was just singing, but I thought it was the radio.

I said, "Is that the radio?"

No one said a word. They were all just smiling, so my son leaned down to my ear, and he continued to sing.

I stopped what I was doing, and I said, "Trevon, that's you singing." I was in disbelief for a minute, and I listened.

As my daughter continued bobbing her head, she said, "Yes, Momma, that's Trevon. It's not the radio."

My son kept singing to me and smiling, and I hugged him, and I said, "I'm so proud of you." I was in tears. My heart was melting with happiness all inside. I was so excited.

I started making plans for my son's music career. After he made his first CD, I went to the day care center, and I let everyone listen to it. I was just that proud of what he had accomplished. I had a small studio built behind my house so that my son could continue to develop his craft daily. I was intrigued at what I was watching him do. He taught himself how to use Pro Tools 12. He would write his own lyrics. He would go in the booth and produce his own CDs. He really put a lot of time into his craft, and he was a perfectionist; if it wasn't perfect to him, he wasn't going to put it out for the public.

I envision my son making it in the music industry. Stage name Trevon Marcel, I went out and I got him a publicist from Atlanta Georgia. She was amazing. I began to come out of my shell. I felt like a new person on a new venture with a new chapter to write in my life. I started investing into his music career. We were entering him into music contests. I wasn't sitting on the back porch anymore. I got a new job, a new business. I'm my son's manager. We got an attorney and formed SOA Entertainment, LLC. I set him up with BMI music group, and I would purchase his beat, copyright, and register his music. That's how he would get paid for his music streams like TuneCore and other music sites.

His PR, I mean this lady got us put in places that you could only dream of. We have rubbed shoulders with some of the biggest names in the music industry and on the reality TV shows. We were on one episode of *Hip Hop* in Atlanta. I mean things were going so good for him. His music made it to the radio stations. He had a couple radio interviews. It's just like we're waiting for his music career to take off. He's shown that he can do it. His sound is unique. He can sing, rap, and he can change his voice up—you wouldn't even believe that it was him on the other end. You would think that he's collaborating with another artist.

We were confident in what we were doing. We have started traveling to Atlanta, Texas, Montgomery, and other places across the South. I started to find myself getting lost in my new world. I knew the day care was good because I had a damn good director and I had a damn good staff, so I wasn't worried about my day care; and when my trailers needed to be attended to, I had a maintenance person that I could always call on if any of my mobile homes needed work. So now I was barely at the day care. Atlanta was the hot spot; it was the place to be. My son's PR would place him at all kinds of celebrity events; and sometimes, when she scheduled him for events, she would give us short notice.

. I was seeing my husband less, and I was hanging out more with my son and the other artists that we had signed to SOA label. My son was making big moves in the music industry, but he still hasn't gotten signed yet. We're doing everything that it takes to get signed. He collaborated with Moneybagg Yo, which was a big deal because he had just gotten signed to a big record label. I was sitting on my back porch, and God spoke to me. It was like someone was sitting with me. He said, as clear as clear can be, "Get ready to prepare yourself and your children."

I felt that warning to my soul. I didn't question what was told to me. I processed the information, and another message came to me: "You won't have that day care for long." That's when I went to my girls first, and I told them, "Whatever you have planned for your life, go ahead and try to accomplish it now while I can help you. I don't know how long I will have the day care."

My girls didn't ask any questions. They both enrolled back in school and got their degrees in their chosen field. I went to my son, and I said, "Trevon, give this music thing all you got. Do whatever it takes to make it. I'm going to help you as much as I can, as long as I can, because I don't know how long I'm going to be in the day care business."

I talked to my children about taking over the business. My son was the only one that showed any interest, but my girls were like, "Momma, I can't take what you take off these people. It's just too much drama going on. I can't do it."

Without letting them know that God had spoken to me, I did inform them and made them aware of my feelings and not to take the message lightly, which I don't think my son really took what I was saying seriously. The more I wasn't at home with my husband, the more it divided us. As a couple, the less I saw my husband, the less I cared if I saw him or not. I didn't care if I communicated with him or not. The feelings I had for him were diminishing. I was losing the love that I once had; it didn't bother me. For once in my life, I feel free, I feel at ease, and I feel like I can be this independent woman who doesn't need a husband to define who I am.

Then my friend Toya and I were sitting at my kitchen table one night, and really, this was her dream; I just wanted to be a part of it. We talked about having a dance team like Diana Williams DD4L, so we named our team that same night Opelika Dancing Stars, and I told her, "Toya, I have the children at the day care who probably want to sign up to be on the dance team. We can start with them," and we watched it grow. Every afternoon after Toya would get off work, she would use a room in the back of the day care that was available for her, and she would teach the children how to dance. She used YouTube and other social media sites to help her develop the skills needed to help teach them to learn how to dance. We were very excited about this team.

It was really stressing Toya out having to juggle work and to make sure her disabled brother was taken care of. It was stretching her thin, so we decided to hire a dance coach to help Toya out. We went through about two or three girls before we got this lady that we thought would be perfect for the team. Toya had already made up a routine, and the only thing she had to do was come and critique the routine just to make it a little better. As time went by, it seemed like everything was perfect with the dance teams. We were filming it with my camera guy. The girls were winning trophies like crazy. Life was good. I told Toya, "I'm going to be involved in this dance team as much as I can."

Remember, I will be traveling with my son when he's traveling with his music, so we had made an agreement, and we understood my role in both situations. We had built a brand. We had a Facebook page. We were building a website the parents paid fees so we could pay for uniforms. We sold food plates to help pay for uniforms and travel expense, and we had teenage parties so we could raise money for anything we needed when it came to the dancers on our team having everything. This team was well known. We built a brand which had lots of girls wanting to join our team. So as all of this is continuing to be a success, we decided to hire a second dance coach to help relieve some of the stress that Toya was going through.

Bad mistake. You know how oil and water don't mix, but when you put them together, the oil is going to come up first because that's the one that has the most force behind it. That's what these two coaches were. You wouldn't think they had anything in common other than dance, but when a bad apple is placed in a perfect basket of apples, it ends up spoiling the whole bunch—just vindictive. You can't trust a soul in this town. You are talking about some envious people—this town is full of them. Your livelihood doesn't mean shit to them; all they want to do is laugh about another person's downfall but continue to live and see what life has in store for you. Laughter is contagious, and sometimes the shoe will be out on the other foot. Do you think you can handle the problems that I have endured?

My stress level is beyond the roof. I'm a praying person, and I'm looking for God to show up in these difficult times I'm going through. I mean this day care is going to kill me. I can't keep going like this—not getting any sleep at night, worrying all the time. Yes, I look happy, but inside I'm dying. Lord, you said you wouldn't put no more on me than I could bear. I didn't realize how much I could hold inside my body until everything is being thrown at me including the kitchen sink. So I'm still having trouble at the day care center. My world was falling apart with the day care center consistently being accused of abusing kids, even accused one of my male employees of molesting a child—they couldn't get their lie straight on that one. So when we spoke to the grandparent, I said, "You are telling me that my employee performs this act in front of other children, and I know he isn't this monster that you are claiming that he is." It was obvious that this plot is bigger than I ever imagine, someone want blood, my life, and my business. The coconspirator behind this accusation is being pushed by some powerful people who wants me out. I couldn't stop dwelling on the fact that if I wouldn't have let this guy do my taxes, he was playing both sides of the fence.

One of his workers told me, "Cynthia, I can't continue to work for someone who tells me to not do your taxes. Just let her think you have done her taxes."

I was told that he was a low-down person. I can't believe that I allowed myself to even do business with this snake. I can just imagine how he was just laughing about me behind my back. He surrounds himself with White people—that's how he continues to stay afloat. One day his float is going to sink because one thing about karma is it's a bitch. Black people in a money-making position do not want to see you accomplish what they have accomplished in their life, but life alert—I have already accomplished success. If y'all don't want me in the building, just say that. You don't have to try to destroy me in the process.

This man has met with me in my face and said, "I'm going to make sure everything goes right between you and the building owners of the day care." Then he went back and told them what I make a year, and they went up on my rent. I was definitely warned about this person—that he was a weasel, a manipulator, a worm, and the scum of the earth. They say he will do anything for money. He was doing the opposite of what he told me—selling your soul to the devil for what? Just to say, "We took her to court. We got her out of our building." No one will bring you the business that God allowed me to bring; you definitely don't know God's chosen people.

Beware of wolves in sheep's clothing. You think you have escaped God's fury, but you haven't. I was all fed up with day care and people because I felt like all of this drama cannot keep happening to one person. What am I doing wrong? Why does the devil have his claws in me? I'm not perfect, but God gave me a damn good heart, and you know what they say—bad things happen to good people. It's ominous that my life is being set up to end bad.

When 2018 was officially here, I wasn't happy about the new year because I knew I was going to have new problems. So I decided to go on Facebook one night and informed everyone that I am closing the day care center and I am selling everything. Boy, that got everyone's attention, and people started contacting me. I was serious, but I did think about my employees and the children I had enrolled—as usual, I'm thinking about everyone else. I should have gone with my first thought, but after talking with two of my employees, we came to a conclusion that I would stay open.

Through all this chaos, I was working diligently to find out who my father was. I went and spoke to a gentleman that the street committee said was my father. I asked him, as hard as it was for me to do that. He said, "Baby, no, I'm not your dad. Me and your mom never had a relationship together, but I hope you find out who he is."

I was heartbroken, but I must continue until I find out who he is. So then I went to a gentleman's house that I was told he was one of my mother's customers when she bootlegs at her house. He mentioned the guys that would go with him to her house to buy whiskey. That conversation with him didn't lead me any further than I already was. So one afternoon I was hanging out with my friend Toya, and we were discussing my situation with me not knowing my father and how I was seeking to find him. I wanted to know, was he still alive? I wanted to know who the man was besides God who created me.

So my friend Toya mentioned, "Send a sample of your saliva to Ancestry.com."

I went ahead, and I purchased the kit. I sent my saliva in. When I got the results back, which was downloaded to my computer, I was amazed and shocked by the names that populated because I have known these people just about all my life. My family has been here all this time without knowing we were family. My bloodline is Brummitt, Farrow, Mosley, Fargason. I was like, "No way. That's why I never liked Terry when he tried to talk to me in school. We are cousins, and Traci is my classmate."

I was blown away. Now how am I going to ask these people for a saliva sample. I was scared. Everyone I got in touch with led me back to Camphill, so I got the nerve up to call and ask about a man supplying his sample so I could find out about my father. Thank God, a man was willing to do it. When we got the results back from 23andMe, we both submitted a sample. He indeed was my uncle. Thank God, I found my family. I was overjoyed because he could have said no, but he allowed me a chance to know who I came from. No more searching. No more wondering. God said I would find out who my earthly father was, that's why I never doubt him, and he's always on time.

When my mother's children found out who my family was, they had a fit. They were saying. "Those people are not your relatives."

My mother wasn't a whore, and I told them, "This is not about her. She is a lady, like any other lady, who had sex with a couple of men and didn't know who her baby daddy is. It's about me, the child. I want to know my bloodline. You all can accept whoever she told you, your father is, but my DNA results told me that Travis was not my father. So whether you want to believe it or not, this DNA test I took with my uncle is true."

I said, "Y'all need to take a DNA test and find out who your daddy is and leave me the hell alone."

They talked about me so bad that I had to post the results on Facebook to shut their mouth up. Once I did that, I didn't hear anything else about my father again. Every child deserves to know their real parents—that shouldn't be taken from anyone. It's my right and my children's right to know as well. I wasn't going to let anyone take that away from us, and I am truly happy knowing who my relatives are, and they invited me into their family with open arms, and for that I am grateful. Day care and life must go on. Lord, have mercy. I keep having this anticipatory anxiety constantly. I'm all fed up with paying people for incidents that happens at the day care, for my day care to always be criticized on Facebook, all the rumors in the streets, everyone talking about, "You know, her day care is under investigation." Of course, it is because y'all can't keep your mouth shut, just waiting on a tragedy to occur.

One of my nieces was employed as a van driver at the day care. It is known to our family that she has mental issues. I have let her stay at my home on several occasions when she relapses from her condition. I know when she's depressed and when she's anxious, she starts to act irrational. She starts to say all kinds of crazy stuff and talking all out of her head with foolishness. Nothing she is saying is making any sense, and the entire family starts to notice her behavior, and we say, "Okay, her schizophrenia is kicking in. So let's keep an eye on her."

My director and a couple of the workers who knew the signs of her condition came to me and let me know that it might not be safe for her to drive the kids right now because of an incident that she told them that had happened on the van.

I called her in the office to talk to her about the incident on the van. First, I asked her, "Is it true that a child opened the door to the van while you were driving?"

She said, "Yes, that's true."

I also asked her, "Do you have control of the children while you're driving the van?"

She said, "No, they do not listen to me."

I told her, "I said if you're having these problems with the children while you are driving, it's very unsafe and can be detrimental. You must be in control of the kids and the van all at the same time."

"But, Auntie, these children are getting on my nerves because they don't listen to me every time. I say something to them, they talk back. I don't know what to do anymore."

"First, you should have come to me and let me know that you were having these problems. I'm noticing that you're starting to shake. That is one of the signs that you have when you're having mental problems. You and your husband are not on the best terms right now, so maybe you just need to stay at home for a little while and get some rest and get yourself together, and make sure you are taking your medication. You know this is very unsafe, and I must protect the children. You're driving people—children—daily. What if you have an accident? Or what if one of the kids jumps off the van? All our asses will be in trouble. Look, right now, I going to suspend you. I am not firing you, okay."

She agreed to everything I said to her. "Keep me informed on how you are doing. You need at least a month to get yourself together." I thought everything between me and her was solved after she left out of my office.

I did not know that she walked around to the other side of the building where my other niece was working and said, "Auntie just fired me. You better look for you another job because you are next." Then she walked around to the other side of the building, telling everyone that I just fired her and "All y'all need to find you another job. She ain't no good. She fired me. She let me go. Y'all know she is under investigation, and I hope they close her damn day care down."

This was a big day care center with two sides, so I didn't hear her at all because I was in my office, and no one told me this until she left the building. I said, "Ungrateful bitch, remember, God doesn't like ugly, and don't—I repeat—mess with his chosen people."

Not a month later, this girl, my niece, came to the day care early one morning. She was clearly on a mission to and a path of destruction. They said she was driving fast acting irrational, just talking crazy. This girl left my day care center and was driving up the road. I don't know what happened, but I got a phone call from my sister Carolyn, and she told me, "You know, our niece has just been in a car accident, and she has been hit by an eighteen-wheeler truck, and they're airlifting her to a hospital in Columbus.

I said, "Okay, I'm on my way." I said to myself, *Now, what if I had left her on that van route driving those children? I know I did the right thing.*

When God said, "Take her off that van route," I knew something was going to happen, and I knew that it wasn't going to be good news. Because when you're living your life destructively, bad things are bound to happen.

After she stayed in the hospital for a long time before she was released, her daughter asked me could her mother come and stay with me. She said, "Auntie, you know you're the only one we can count on," so me being the weak link in every situation, I let her come stay with me once again. So I let a friend of mine come stay with us so she could help me with her. We had to give this lady her baths, change her adult diapers like she was an infant all over again, and we stayed on her, encouraging her to walk because I believe she had truly given up on life.

We begged her every day, "Try to push your body so you can get up and walk again," and I encouraged her by saying, "Don't you want to be the person you once were—outgoing—and don't you want to dress up and look pretty?" just anything to give her hope again. I said, "Don't you want to wipe your own body so no one will be looking at you? Don't you want to get out in this world? I know you don't want to be bedbound for the rest of your life."

My sister Carolyn told my sister Annie and Jackie a lie on me at the hospital. She told them that I said I didn't want any of them to come to the hospital to see their niece. Boy, she would tell a lie on you, and then she would hide her hands like she didn't have anything to do with what was going on. And they believed everything that came out of Carolyn's mouth. If she would have told them that the sky was purple when she woke up, knowing that it's blue, they would have said, "Yes, the sky was purple," when Carolyn woke up. Yeah, Carolyn said it, and them damn fools know the sky is blue. It's called manipulation of the mind. Why this lady is still playing games and keeping the family divided was beyond my comprehension. We have been in the day care business for twenty years. When are you going to grow up? I don't have a reason to tell them that they cannot see their niece. "She's not my daughter. I don't care what y'all do. Just leave me alone."

It's funny how family can keep up mess within the family, but when you need them the most, they are never there. I needed them to come up and help change her and help feed her and help do something that could encourage and motivate her to want to live instead of furthering the division that was taking place inside this dysfunctional family. Her father and brothers would come sometimes, but men didn't want to change diapers. Her sister came a couple of times, and her daughter would visit her often; but none of the aunts, uncles, cousins came. You need that family love to make it out of that kind of life-changing tragedy. It was just me and my friend trying to nurse this lady back to health. I needed a break, my friend needed a break, and plus I still had a day care to operate. I still had obligations that I had to do, but I'm always taking on someone else's trouble and problems and making them my on. Never again will I volunteer myself for someone who has close family members that are very capable of helping with the responsibilities of a loved one. You love them until something happens. Now you don't have time.

Her ungrateful daughter said, "I just wanted to be noticed," by helping her mother. Newsbreak—I wasn't given an award. When you, your brother, and your mother had to stay with me because of her illness, I didn't get an award the other two times she had to stay with me for her mental issues, and did she forget she asked me to take on her trouble? There's no notoriety in cleaning shit. She should have been with her daughter from the start, but you don't have time for her, and then you want to blame other people for a job you should be doing. This is just how dysfunctional this family is. They choose to blame everything on someone else just because they don't have the audacity to take it upon their self to be the woman or the man they say they are.

Well, I and her daughter had an argument, and I told her to come get all her momma shit from my house with that nasty attitude she has that doesn't look cute for a young lady with girls to have such a nasty demeanor about herself, so that headache is gone, but I'm still managing my son's career, operating the day care, and taking care of my mobile homes. Through all of this chaos, I'm still in financial stress. I was begging my husband to help me. I told him what I was going through. I explained to him that I was in financial debt and I don't think I'm going to make it. "Can you please help me? We need to borrow some money from somewhere so I can keep these day care centers operating. I need your help."

My cries fell on deaf ears. He had no empathy or mercy for me as always. I was literally sinking. I was in a deep hole, and no one knew it. I was so mad with my husband a month before this tragedy happened in my life. I believe I was going through post-traumatic stress.

I kept asking him, was he going to borrow the money for me? Was he going to help me? And he kept telling me no.

I said, "Are you going to help me refinance the house? How can you say you will not help? You are living in a nice home. You wear nice clothes. I buy you just as much as I buy my children. You're living off the life that I provide. I'm keeping a roof over your head, food on the table."

But he was determined that he wasn't going to help me, and he didn't. So I had to make a way for something to happen for me to hold on to everything that I had. But that last no, I went in my bedroom, and I got my nine-millimeter gun, and I got my Taurus gun loaded—both of them. When he came in the room, I just started shooting both guns one after the other. He ran outside because he was so scared. He thought I was shooting at him. I really wasn't because I could've hit him if I wanted to. I was shooting because of the situation I was in. This fool went outside, and he called the police— the second man to call the police on me in a marriage because you pushed me to that point of no return.

When the police arrived at our home, they asked me where I placed the guns, and I gave the guns to them. Then a paramedic and police officer spoke to me about what was going on, and they decided that I needed to go speak to someone in the psych unit, so when we arrived at the hospital, they did allow a therapist to talk with me and try to help me through that situation I was going through, and he recommended that I get some help. He prescribed medication and told me to follow up with my doctor, and he dismissed me to go home. People shouldn't judge people because no one knows what a person has been through and what goes on in people lives. People can push you to the edge. You can find yourself in a dark place that you never meant to go to.

In 2014, DHR came out with this new system for providers to get paid, which day care providers had to attend and not parents. It didn't make any sense for the meeting to be for day care providers; the state should have been responsible for training their parents that they placed on the program to learn to swipe these cards in and out. Placing the responsibility on the owners of the day care centers was a complete setup, a travesty within itself. We were trained on how to use the cards. They were like, "EBT cards or a debit card?"

Once the parents, grandparents, cousins, friends, or whoever you want to swipe your card could swipe your child in/out if they had your pin, that's how the day care would get paid.

We were told by family guidance and DHR that if we had any problems teaching the parents how to swipe their cards, we could call our local agency, and they would walk us through this process. Why were we given the responsibility by family guidance and DHR as privately owned day care centers to teach their people, who are in their government program, how to swipe in or out with this card? We as privately owned day care centers are not employed by the state of Alabama. The state of Alabama only provides licenses to day care owners.

Family guidance receives federal funds to disburse to low-income families for childcare assistance, and DHR regulates childcare. So why did they place this responsibility on us as daycare providers? All of this was a setup to weed out providers who made a profitable income. We were told in the meeting that if we were caught with the cards, our subsidy would be suspended for six months to a year and that we could reapply for subsidy. We were never told we could be prosecuted because it wasn't a crime. So I wanted to know when it became a crime. No one notified us as providers. The responsibility of training for these cards fell upon family guidance and DHR and not the providers. It was a miscarriage of *justice*, and they know it. And I'm going to expose them for the dirty rats that they are.

As day care providers, we never signed an agreement with family guidance, DHR, nor the state of Alabama saying that we would not keep the parents' cards at the daycare. Family guidance and DHR only said, "We do not want you all as providers to keep the cards that we are providing to the parents." The parents were the only ones who had to sign an agreement with family guidance to not give the cards to the daycare centers. We are not the only day care and will never be the only day care that keep cards. At first, we weren't keeping the parents' cards. We started keeping some of the people that we feel like we could trust, and then some people were just lazy to take the time out of their day to stop by a machine and swipe their child out for the day. Some parents we had to chase down just for them to swipe their children in/out for the whole week. Sometimes we would get cursed out for asking people to come in and swipe your children for five days that they have been here. The only reason I decided to start keeping the cards was because you could not get people to do what they needed to do.

Don't get me wrong—some of the parents did what they needed to do. We wouldn't have a problem with everyone, and some of the parents paid their day care fee without incident and brought everything that their child needed, and some even donated different items to the day care. It's the bad people that spoil everything for everyone else, letting greed take over and people telling them, "You can sue that lady," but in reality, you can't afford a lawyer. It boggles my mind on the influence that other people can have on vulnerable people who are looking for a come up off your success. The complaints to DHR intensified, which made DHR start calling the police to investigate instead of them coming out themselves. The police started taking my drive to my camera system so they can start an investigation into what was going on.

Each time the investigator couldn't find anything, nothing was going on and they would have to give our drive back, and we would continue to work as normal. The DHR worker came out to the facility at least once a week. I think she was getting tired of the complaints herself. "Cynthia, I don't know what's going on. I have to come out when someone calls," and it would be reports that were unfounded.

Someone wanted me out of this building bad, and someone wanted this building for a day care center. They didn't have to go to such drastic lengths to get me out of the building. Really, was it worth destroying my life? How far will a person go to stop your livelihood, to stop you in your tracks, to bring you down, and to tear you apart? It's like a tiger ripping at his prey. One thing I noticed about the state and DHR—no matter what happens at the White day cares, they don't get publicized for the incidents that occurred at their day care center. You never knew what had happened unless a Black employee let the cat out the bag, unless a child died at the hands of a White person because White people take care of their own. They don't go around trying to destroy each other unless they can be directly tied to the event, then they expose the person. We don't operate that way. We are all for ourselves, and if you lose out, oh well.

After I found a new building and I started to invest in this new place, I made the biggest mistake of all. I refinanced the home that was almost paid for to save my business. I invested fifty thousand dollars in this facility for these children to have a day care that I always dreamed of having one day. I had paid for all the repairs. I installed a new fire system, new carpet, new sinks, poured the concrete, placed new toilets for the regulation, which were eleven. So yes, I ended up losing a lot of money in that building. Once this wall started to fall, life as I knew it would never be the same, which led me to the beginning of the end—questioning everything that I truly believed in. Something bigger than life was waiting for me because what I was about to encounter would-be complete destruction. It was the highest level of a weapon used against a person—so many knives in my back. I didn't realize how many people in this small town had their paws in me. The last five years of me being in business, I can't explain the hell I encountered. The complaints were being kept for evidence of the times the police were called to come to my faculty by DHR, I didn't know that this had reached the level of conspiracy that was being formed against me. Everyone was out to get little old me, the person that will give you the shirt off her back. My life changed forever, and Satan was out to take everything that God had given me, and my faith was being challenged. A horrific event was about to unfold that would shock this town and surrounding areas for years and years to come. Satan knew that myself and my sister would be the center point of attention.

Two weeks before this incident occurred, my brother got mad with me about some money. It was an explosive argument. Our arguments don't usually come out well, and he said, "Don't worry, you won't have those day cares for too much longer. January 31, 2019— the day that my life would change forever. My husband and I were sleeping in separate rooms. He was sleeping on one side of the house, and I was sleeping on the other side of the house. I was lying in bed asleep when I heard a hard pound on the door. It was like a tornado was ripping the walls apart. I got up from my bed and stumbled to the door.

I was like, *What the hell is that?* I didn't know what to think. I said, "Who is it?"

Someone replied to me, "Opelika Police Department."

I said, "Who are you looking for? What y'all want? We don't sell drugs."

"Open the door, ma'am. We have a search warrant for Cynthia and Bobby Jones."

My heart dropped. I opened the door, and I said, "You have a search warrant for what?"

Upon the police entering my house, the first person they asked about was the handicap lady in the wheelchair: "Where is she? What room is she in?"

"Who are you talking about? My niece? She doesn't live here anymore."

Instantly, when the police enter your home, you lose all your rights. They immediately consider you a criminal. Then they start telling you what to do. They won't let you move. They make you sit down in one spot until they need you in a room where they are in. Meanwhile they are destroying your room, looking for whatever they are looking for.

When that officer called me in my room, the first thing I asked him was, "What are you looking for? What have we done?"

"Ma'am, we're here looking for anything pertaining to your day care center."

I said, "What you mean 'pertaining to my day care center'?"

My cell phone was ringing off the hook. Everyone in the day care was trying to reach me. The officer would not let me answer the phone.

He said, "I bet you those are your workers at the day care trying to reach you, but I got officers down there too, so don't worry. You don't have to answer the phone. We are looking for cards. Don't you have cards that belong to the people who come to your day care?"

"No, sir, I don't have any cards here."

He continued to search my room and all over my home. I felt so degraded and betrayed and just downright dirty at how they came into our home and invaded our privacy. For what, there was no reason to do all that. Don't y'all have real criminals to arrest?

This smart-mouth officer—you know you always have a jackass out of the bunch—he said, "We could have thrown you to the ground. What you think about that?"

I wanted to spit in his face. I put that shit look on my face, and he knew what that meant. Then they placed me in handcuffs and told me I was under arrest and that I was going with them to the station. The police treat you as if you don't have feelings when they enter your home, like you are beneath them. When my oldest daughter arrived at my house, she saw the police put me in the car. She was screaming for her mother. It broke my heart for my daughter to see me like that. It was a degrading moment for me.

She said, "Where are y'all taking my momma?" She was crying.

I was in disbelief. This could not be real—it had to be a dream. I had never been in real trouble with the law before. Yes, twenty years ago, I got arrested for a DUI, but I'm talking about real crimes. You would have thought that I had committed murder that day by the way I was being treated. I didn't understand until I was arrested. What was really going on? I did not realize that they had invaded my sister's house as well as her day care center. I didn't look at my phone. I didn't watch TV. I was told our pictures were on every TV station, Facebook, and all social media sites that you can name. We were being featured as the sisters in the crime of the century together. I heard that this aired for about two to three weeks. They don't air murderers' photos that many times on television.

The news of our arrest was spreading like wildfire. The whole community acted as if we had just gone in the mall and murdered sixteen people and left all of them dead and then turned around and killed ourselves. So why do we receive so much injustice? I have seen White people working for the government who are accused of stealing money. They don't run their segment repeatedly. You have people who embezzle millions and millions of dollars, and you might hear the story one time. Why? Because they're White. And then the DA had the nerve to have a press conference about us, the sisters. First of all, my sister and I didn't even speak to one another. Someone didn't give him all of his facts. In his press conference, he said he did not know what to do with us because he had never encountered a case like this before.

Then the DA goes on to say, "The day cares won't close. We're not shutting them down, and the cards are not illegal to have at the day cares. They are just frowned upon."

Yet we are charged with having the cards. The ten parents whom I was charged with placing their children on the day care program illegally have actually been on the program for years. Some of them went through DHR, and some signed up through family guidance. These children never miss coming to day care. They even charged me for my two daughters' children, who were enrolled, and they applied through family guidance and got approved on their own without my help. So why are they saying I placed these people on the program? And some of the kids were school age, so they were considered after-school children. So of course, they were signed in for the second shift. I had a lot of after-school children that my drivers pick up from school. I can justify why they are clocked in like they were. You can only clock one child in at a time, so the time is not going to match up to what family guidance or the state is claiming. I was told by a state employee that they have had other day care centers found with the cards, but they weren't brought up on charges. They were suspended for a period of time, place off suspension, and then able to receive subsidies again. So when I spoke with the investigator who oversaw the investigation—he was the one who always investigated the incidents that occurred at my day care center—he told me I was being charged with twelve counts of fraud, and each count carried a ten-year sentence, and my sister was being charged with eleven counts of fraud, which also carried a ten-year sentence each. We were told that we would pay back one hundred sixty thousand dollars each. My sister paid hers off with no problem because they took all the money that she had out of her bank account, and they paid DHR back. I didn't have that type of money in my account, so I was set up on a payment plan for money that I made legally and the girl who worked for family guidance, who they said was placing kids in our day care center. I guess she received immunity, which was not fair to us. Because we didn't work for Family Guidance—she did—she didn't receive any punishment.

If she placed kids at our day care, then she placed them in all the day cares because the Family Guidance workers would often ask you if you have an opening for children. So that was a lie that she only called us, and also, we didn't have access to their computers. Why wasn't she held accountable? Because her mother worked for the State of Alabama. This is injustice. You are talking about a life-changing event, not knowing what your future has in store for you. After hiring a local attorney, I could feel in my spirit that he was a good person who was going to do the best job that he could to defend me. I was in meetings with him on several occasions and went alone except for once when my director went with me. This was a very lonely process that I went through. My attorney believed in me and what I shared with him. On one of my visits, he told me, "Cynthia, this is Lee County, a mostly White town. What if you get a jury that's all White? They're going to find you guilty. I don't trust the people in this town, and I don't want you to put your life on the line when you can take this plea bargain and live your life."

It took some time for him and my son to convince me of this, but I knew that I didn't want to spend fifty years of my life in prison for being a person who honestly was just out to help other people, and the payback in return is my livelihood being taken away from me.

My means of making money, my way of life has just been destroyed. So I took the plea bargain. Until this day, I'm still not comfortable with the decision I made and the charges that was brought against me. The plea bargain consisted of six counts of fraud and pay restitution with five years' probation. To me, that's still not justice because I wanted to go to court and fight my case. I felt like I was in a fog, I felt like this wasn't happening to me and that this wasn't supposed to happen to me. I'd never accepted the situation that I was in because I felt like God would save me, that he had something special waiting on me in my life. I was telling God to come and save me, save me from these destructive vessels of the devourer. Jail was something I never accepted because God said, "You're not going. I have other plans for you. You've got to have more than mustard seed faith to go through this typhoon that you're about to go through."

When I was released from jail, I realized every event that happened at my day care center, every time DHR took a parent of a child to the police department to try to bring charges against someone or myself, every scar on a child or if a child fell while playing with a toy at my facility, or any little thing you could imagine—all those complaints from the public, whether it was true or false, when DHR told parents that if they were placing their child/children at my day care, they weren't going to pay for the services. This was personal. This was not because of incidents. They wanted me close for some reason. I was now going to pay the price for everything. I couldn't handle it. I knew what it felt like to be accused of a crime. But this time, DHR wanted blood, and they were going to get it. Another wall was taken down in my life. My husband and I said wedding vows—for better or for worse, in sickness and in health, until death do us part, that we would travel through any storm together no matter what—but he left me at the worst time of my life, and I had a hard time forgiving him for that. I had court appearances; he didn't ask about them. He didn't show up—not one time. I went to court all alone, having to deal with this situation all by myself. Maybe you would say I got in this trouble all by myself, but I'm married, and if no one was there, he should have been by my side. All those friends I thought I had—

no one was there to be found. My telephone that rang off the hook 24-7 now has stopped ringing.

No one organized a fundraiser for me. No one made a GoFundMe account. No one asked me if I needed help in any type of way. When people show you who they are, believe them now. For once I knew the truth about how people really felt. I had fallen from grace, and no one cared. I would stay in my bedroom all day long and close my curtains. I kept my room as dark as possible, and all I did was cry. I hardly got out of bed to get something to eat. I feel so alone for the first time in my life. The people that I considered my family because my real family didn't accept me—they didn't even call.

I said, "God, don't fail me. Everyone else has left me. Please, God, don't leave me. If you leave me, I will have nobody." I prayed so much until I had no more tears to cry. People who were truly my friends, they stayed by my side, and they kept encouraging me. I even had a classmate from school, Tammy, reach out to me. That's what people are supposed to do in your time of need, but I could count on one hand the ones that stuck by my side. They always say you never know people until you need them or until something happens to you. That's when you find out your true friends—that's the realist statement I was taught during this situation how people will change up on you when the money is gone. When they don't need you anymore, when they don't have to call and ask you for a favor, they turn their backs on you because—guess what—they were never there from the start. It was all a façade. It was all because of what you had and who you were.

When I went before the judge all alone—just me and my attorney—it still didn't seem real. It still seemed as if I was in a dream. As I and the attorney approached the bench, I was crying. Every count he read, I really didn't hear him. I was crying and focusing on the Lord.

My attorney spoke to me and said, "Cynthia, are you still here with me? Are you listening?" And I nodded yes with tears in my eyes. I have never felt so degraded in my whole entire life standing there before a judge and having to give up all my rights as a citizen. Everything that I have ever known, the person that I had become, left that day. Cynthia is no more. She is gone. That person that I was, she is gone. She is here no longer. She is not here to be played upon. Cynthia is not here anymore to be judged and her name to be scandalized. She is not here to be taken advantage of. She is not here anymore to help the people in need. She is not here anymore to help soothe your pain. She's not here anymore to help other people with their problems. She's not here anymore to give to others before thinking of herself first. That person left that day, and she will never return. After I'm trying to continue to live my life and keep my center open, I couldn't feel anything—not even my heartbeat. I thought I would wake up from this nightmare, this horrible nightmare, but I didn't because it was real, and it was getting worse. Not only was I broken financially, I was breaking spiritually, but I couldn't let go of God. He was my only hope. The praying person that I am and my faith in God—that was all I had left.

My life was slipping away from me. The overwhelming gossip was getting to me. Who I am as a person was being questioned. I didn't know what to do. People didn't know I was drowning in financial debt. I was on the brink of losing it all. I was living a lie. I had borrowed money from every loan company that would let me have a loan. I had run up all my credit cards. I had spent all the money that I had saved. I had a 700 credit score. I had exhausted all my financial resources. People said I spent all my money on my son's career—that's a lie. I was already drowning in debt when he started his career. No one knew my financial situation because it wasn't their business, but I made success look good, and I was successful. I had handled this financial burden for over twenty years. I had gotten used to it, but somehow it got out of hand. It was out of control, and without subsidy, I wouldn't be able to keep the daycare doors open, and the state knew that. That's why they didn't close the centers; they knew without subsidy, we would not be able to stay open.

I tried as long as I could to save the two day care centers, but I was fighting a losing battle, and it hurt me to find out that some of my employees who had worked for me ten years or more didn't even want people to know that they work for me. They were ashamed. You weren't ashamed when life was good. That's how people treat you when you get in trouble—they disassociate themselves from you. It is really a shame because everyone in this town knows who has worked for me and who was working for me at the time of the incident. I was beyond disappointed in that statement. What you call home— now you are ashamed to be associated with. That put me in a deeper depression, in a deeper downhill spiral. After I closed both day care centers, I started to sell off items that I cherished; I worked so hard to acquire all my belongings. I had to sell all ten vans to survive. I had to let someone else take over the day care that I spent fifty thousand dollars on repairing. I had to sell everything I could just to stay afloat. All this turmoil I'm thinking, what do my children think of me? Are they still proud of me? I felt like a failure to my children and my grandchildren. I always wanted to leave them something in this life after I'm gone that no one was able to leave me. I wanted them to see a mom who was strong, independent, intelligent, determined, and ambitious, a motivated person who never gave up on her dreams. I wanted to close with dignity and to do it on my terms, not in disgrace. I didn't know how they felt, but I was going to find out.

It's funny how life throws you a curveball when you least expect it. Now I'm having to learn how to live poor. Even though I was struggling with my businesses, I still had money put away. I could still use credit cards. I still could get small loans. We were still living comfortably. This is something that affected my children. When this situation happened to me, it happened to them as well. It affected my children; they're used to living a certain lifestyle like I'm used to living a certain lifestyle. You can imagine being able to go out and purchase almost anything you want and not having to save up for it; being able to get it that same day, whip it in a bag, place it in your arms, and walk out the store with it anytime you like. Now I'm having to go to stores that I've never shopped in before—the Penny Annie stores. I got to check the prices on the items; I might have a five-dollar bill, and I got to go in this store and come out with five dollars' worth of items.

It took some time to get used to living that way. I did the best that I could as I shop for these items that were $0.50 or $1.00. It was very hard for me to wrap my head around this life. I couldn't believe all that I had was gone. This was so hard for me, not to mention my kids and my grandkids because they depended on me—the only person who was there for them. I felt like such a failure, having to look in their face and admit that Mama fucked up, and I'm so sorry. I'm wondering what they thought about me daily—the person they admired, the person that they looked up to, who had fallen from grace—so I had to find something to do every day to keep me motivated and occupied my mind, and I started to get back into helping Toya with the dance team. We were still going two competitions while I still had a couple of vans, but we didn't have any place to practice anymore. We had to start using the local gym. We were still raising the money for the children so that we could afford to take them out of town to dance competitions and purchase uniforms.

Little did we know that behind our back, the coaches were conspiring to steal the team, and the parents knew it. On the last cookout that we had for the kids, Toya and I had worked tirelessly on the grill and cooked fish for the upcoming uniforms that we were going to buy for the kids. We raised about one thousand two hundred dollars that day, but I noticed that when the coach came to the event, she didn't speak to me. The other coach was across the street because he was making a video that day, but the plot that they had was all taking place behind my and Toya's back. Some of the parents were acting funny because they knew that they had decided to betray us and leave our team. We would have felt better if they would have come to us and said, "Cynthia, Toya, we feel like you all are not going to be able to help coach our girls anymore because we understand Ms. Cynthia has some issues that she is going through right now. So we decided to pull away from you all," but naw, the coach that we hired had the audacity to create a group chat explaining how she woke up one day and decided she wanted her own dance team but she didn't find her own children, explaining how all of the children decided to follow her. It wasn't the children's idea; it was the grown-up's idea that you're taking the entire team. I think that was very dirty and low-down.

They went out and told everyone that I stole the one thousand two hundred dollars. How can I steal my own money? They did not put a helping hand into what went on that day, and when they called and asked me for the money, no, I don't care who you are, y'all stole the team. Get out and raise the money like we did. Hustle for what you want. You won't take the money like you took the team. Never take something that doesn't belong to you because it might not work out the way you want it to.

I told Toya, "Don't worry about them. God will handle this as well." What we don't understand is that you can have faith and belief plus trust in the Lord our God, but the flesh is weak in all circumstances, which leads us to still have doubt that we don't want to admit to. Until we fix that flesh which guides all aspects of our lives, we would never have that relationship with God that we truly desire. You see, it is the flesh that holds us back. No matter who you are or where you come from, until you fix your flesh, we will always fall short of the glory and the true divine blessings of the Lord that we are all seeking. My flesh was weak.

I was wondering what has become of my life. Why has God forsaken me? He promised not to leave me, yet I feel he isn't there along with all of the people.

My sister Carolyn would often stop by to check on me, and she told me, "Cynthia, you've got to get out of this bed. You can't keep living like this. You are going to keep sinking deeper and deeper into depression, and stress will kill you. Look at me. I didn't let anything stop me."

You know my sister Carolyn, she thinks she's the baddest woman in town. She said, "I wish a motherfucker would approach me about this shit because I will beat some asses"—and for real she would. But I wasn't her. I wasn't that strong—I was weak. I was that weak little girl who had big dreams, and once those dreams had shattered, I was nobody all over again. I still don't want to be seen by people. I'm still letting the rumors and gossip hold me back because the flesh is weak. The shame and guilt that I felt, the disappointment that I had become to my children all the years that I had accomplished, I felt like it all had been wasted. Why couldn't I just be a regular worker? Get a regular paycheck week by week? Why did I have to want more in life? Why did I have to be an entrepreneur? Why did I have to have all these goals that had to be accomplished in my life? Why was I a dreamer? Why have I wanted more? Why couldn't I just live the little simple life that most people live but that wasn't for me, the simple life?

I desired more. I wanted more. I felt like I was special—not that I'm special over others but that special feeling that you have inside about yourself if you don't have that feeling. I can't explain it to you. It's a feeling that God gives you. I'm one of those people I'd never thought that I couldn't have the desires of my heart, that the world is my oyster, and that we can have what we ask God for. I sank deeper and deeper into depression, not wanting to live in this town anymore, not wanting to see the people here, not wanting to be around anyone. Everything was gone that I ever worked for the day care and the dance team. Thank God I still had my mobile homes to live off, but the income doesn't supplement or replace the income that the day care brought in, so I was back to struggling. My bills outweighed the income that the mobile homes brought in. I felt like my house had been invaded by evil people. I wasn't comfortable in my safe haven anymore. It felt dirty. It didn't feel like home anymore.

I should have been that person that had stopped letting people use me, but no, I'm still giving and giving and giving, and they're taking and taking and taking, and no one cares or gives a damn about me. But now, I'm that person that is needing help. When you ask family members for money and you don't hear back from them and it seems as if they are avoiding you, and when my husband asked my sister Jackie to help me with paying my attorney, she replied, "That's your wife. She didn't deal with us anyway. No, I can't help her." At some point, family should set their differences aside when it comes to a traumatic event. I explained to Bobby when he asked me about asking my family to help me financially. I said, "No, don't ask any of them." But he didn't listen; he just reconfirmed what I knew my whole life. I was done. Every setback is a setup for a comeback. I was ready to leave Alabama. I needed a fresh start. I needed a new beginning, and I thought that I could do that. When I was telling my family that I was going to Georgia, everyone wanted to follow me. I didn't beg anyone to go—they wanted to go on their own—but like the old sayings say, when you do something, always do it by yourself. Never invite anyone no matter how much you love them. Some battles are meant to be fought alone.

Okay, I have decided that I would move to Georgia just to get away. No, I'm not running from anybody or anyone; I needed that time away from it all. I needed that space from Opelika because every time I passed a day care center, my heart would ache. I would cry day after day, so I felt like if I moved away, everything would be different; I would feel better. But sure enough, I'm old enough to know that the pain doesn't stop just because you move, but I wanted to give it a try anyway. Maybe I can restart my life there. Maybe, just maybe, it can be better for me. There I was thinking new state, new city, new life, new me, not knowing that I would have bigger problems following me to this new city. A felony was one of them, and my mental state was the other.

All my children wanted to follow me to Georgia. I think the situation that I went through had affected them to the point where they weren't ashamed but fed up and they would rather move out of town and not deal with it. So my three children and my daughter's husband all decided to go since my granddaughter wasn't on my and Toya's dance team anymore because it was stolen. My daughter and I discussed letting her try out for Miss Diana's team in Atlanta because she loves to dance. Somehow my son-in-law's mother decided that she wanted to move when we move. This was new information to me because I wasn't expecting her to be among us, but I didn't have a problem with it.

Every other day, my daughter or my son-in-law's mother contacted me, asking me had I found a house. They just kept worrying me about finding a house in Georgia. So on a couple of occasions, we drove up to view a couple of homes that I had found, and we decided on the one we wanted, and we were approved for it. I took the money that I made from the items that were sold from the day care and I made the down payment on the house.

Why don't I listen to what God tells me? He told me that it wasn't going to work. Everyone is grown. The old saying is you can't have too many grown people under one roof. When I tell you God always warns me, he does. I'm going to learn one day to obey God when he speaks to me. Everything God has told me and warned me about has come to pass. So before we moved, I thought everything was good. I was told that we were going to have a meeting before we all moved to Georgia so that everyone would have a clear understanding of the role they would play while we lived together, and everyone would pitch in and pay their part, which was understandable.

I didn't have a problem with the meeting; it's what happened during the meeting. We were getting ready to have the meeting, and everyone was there—my oldest daughter, my son, my godson, my middle daughter, her husband, and his mother. The vibe in the room was off. My discernment was kicking in. Something wasn't right. This seemed like a setup. Rule number 1: When you make plans, don't involve family.

My son-in-law and my son knew each other before my daughter met him. Anytime I wanted to talk to him about my son, he always would give me advice because they called each other brothers, and I knew my son respected him enough to listen to his advice. We mostly talked about my son's music career as an upcoming rap artist. My son-in-law would always keep my son encouraged on his music, encouraging him to stay focused and "Don't stop. Keep writing and performing."

My son-in-law seemed to have a chip on his shoulders. He seemed arrogant and bold. I had never seen him like that before. So as the meeting transpired, the tension grew in the room. My son-in-law said to my son, "What are your intentions once we get to Georgia?"

My son replied, "I'm going to get a job. What you think?" Then he asked my godson, "What're your intentions?"

My godson replied, "I'm going to get a job too and help," and then my son-in-law started to become demanding like he was the authoritarian and as if he was throwing his weight around with his words to intimidate them. It only made my son grow angry, and then the argument got heated, and that's when the altercation began. We ladies couldn't stop them. We tried. My godson was able to get my son out the house so they could gather their composure.

My son-in-law's mother immediately said, "I can't do this."

I had never seen a person give up so fast right then and there with no questions asked, no reason why other than "If this is what's going to go on in Georgia, I can't be a part of it." That's the setup right there. That's how you take yourself out of the agreement—she knew she wasn't going in the first place.

None of us want to be a part of grown-ups fussing, fighting, and arguing among each other. You're not the only one, so since I got this money all tied up in this house—all six of our names are on the lease—I got to move regardless of whether I want to move or not. But everyone else really does have a choice to stay except for me, then I realized I made another mistake by putting all my money into moving because it truly was a mistake, and from that day on, it didn't get any better. This was going to be a disaster. He clearly wasn't ready to move either, and he would prove it sooner than anyone could imagine. We all moved except his mother.

When we pulled up to our new home in Suwanee, Georgia, which was an upscale community, as we were unpacking the U-Haul truck and our vehicles, a Caucasian lady appeared in our yard and walked up to us and introduced herself.

She said, "I'm CJ from across the street." So I started to introduce all the members of my family. After that, she immediately started to ask, "Where are you all from? How did you find Suwanee?" and was telling us how long she had been living in the community. Before I could answer any of her questions, she would ask another one. Then she said, "What's you all story?" as I gasped to catch my breath. She started to say what they don't allow in the neighborhood. She said she is a part of the neighborhood watch and she keeps her eyes on everything that goes on in the community, and she kept referring to the other people that live there, which didn't make sense to me because we didn't know them.

I said with authority, "We are not drug dealers," as I was getting ready to cuss her ass out.

My husband, Bobby, said, "Hey, Cynt, I need you over here."

I was getting ready to have a Cindy moment. We all said, "We are going to have some trouble out of this lady."

I replied, "She doesn't want these problems," as she went back across the street.

We had settled in our new home. After about a month, my son-in-law left my daughter. She was pregnant, and they already had a daughter. I couldn't believe what he had just done. I would never look at him the same. Everyone was getting along good. There had not been any more arguments, no fussing, so I couldn't understand how he could leave his wife, daughter, and unborn son, but it wasn't for me to figure out. My daughter was never happy after her husband left. She distanced herself. She became grumpy and didn't want to be around anyone. She had changed. It seemed as if she didn't like any of us. She became selfish and withdrawn. This was not the smiling, cheerful daughter that I know who had such a calm spirit, the one person that I could always count on who always had my back. Her words would speak volumes I had never heard before, and that would break my heart.

I thought it was because of the pregnancy, and I do believe that was a part of it, but it was also because they had decided to move, and I think that he convinced her that it was a mistake, but I also think that he convinced her that it was all my fault. The arguments between my children were getting the best of me. One thing I have always wanted for my children was to love one another and get along with one another. It's not uncommon for siblings to fuss, but I did not want them to become me, the relationship that I didn't have with my family. I wanted them to visit one another, to look out for one another, to be there for each other. I'm trying to grasp hold of the transition of moving and the fact that we are here. We really moved in this bitch. Across the street, CJ is turning up the heat. I was sitting on the front step one day, and I was looking across the street at CJ's house, and I noticed that a camera was in her window pointing straight across the street at us. I told everyone that lived in the house to be careful because it's a camera pointing right at us from CJ's house. "Don't let her see y'all do anything that you shouldn't be doing." I didn't trust her, but I was thinking that it had something to do with the neighbors that lived there before us, but she didn't take it down. She left it so she could watch our every move. Then she started to leave letters on our cars; I knew about the first letter. Not one time when she had a party did I complain about her guest blocking the driveways, preventing us from backing out, but her letter spoke of us blocking her from backing out. We didn't have company because we didn't know anyone in this town. We had five cars. Two were in the garage, two were outside the garage, and my nephew would park on the curve, but he would not block her from backing out of her driveway.

Then I started to get letters from HOA, and they would talk about our grass needing to be cut, and if it wasn't cut by a certain date, we would be fined twenty-five dollars. So I went out and I purchased a lawn mower, and I would keep the grass cut. That wasn't enough for CJ because I figured out she was reporting us. One day my daughter Kendra said, "Come here, Mama, hurry up. Come look. Someone is parked out front of the house taking pictures. Shortly after that, I got another letter from HOA. I knew it was that chick CJ reporting us for something. They were talking about the upkeep of the house. Nowhere in my contract did it say I need to paint the front of the house. I did keep the bushes trimmed in front of the yard. The guy next door told me about the trash can going back in the garage after it has been picked up, but he said it in a very nice way.

He said, "I was just letting you know in case you didn't know."

I replied to him, "Thank you," because I didn't know I come from the country where you can leave your trash can outside your house as long as you like, but I knew I was in a different type of community, and I was willing to obey the rules.

But CJ was still being sneaky and up to her old tricks until my nephew Petro was fed up.

He said, "Auntie, I didn't want to tell you, but I got to because I'm mad now. The lady across the street is still leaving letters on our cars. I just remove them, so you want read them because I know how you are. The letters are getting a little more demanding and out of hand. I was hiding the letters from you because I didn't want you to get in any trouble, and I know right now this is something that you don't need to have to deal with on top of everything else that is going on."

I said, "You didn't have to hide the letters from me, but we're going to handle this today," and he begged me to let him go over there and talk to her.

He said, "Auntie, you stay here. You don't need to go."

I said, "Oh yeah, I'm going. It's going to take me to stop her." He gathered up all the letters that he had kept, and he gave them to me.

A ball of fire was in the pit of my stomach. I said, "Let's go. It's time for me to give this bitch a dose of Cindy."

I started walking fast—that's what I do when I get mad. My nephew was walking behind me, talking about, "Don't go over there and act a fool." Now you know this is exactly what I'm going to do act a fool.

I said, "Boy, shut up. I got this. Come on."

We knocked on the door, and CJ answered. I was mad as hell, and I know she could feel it.

I told her, "As many parties you have been having since we have been here, you block us from backing out of our driveway, and no one says anything to you about it. I'm just now finding out about these letters that you've been leaving on our cars. As far as these letters, they belong to you. Here you go."

She said, "No, they're yours. You can keep them."

I dropped them to her feet, and I said, "They're yours. You keep them."

That made her so angry, but she couldn't keep up with this mouthpiece that I got. Her husband came to the door after hearing all the commotion. He just looked and didn't say one word. He was looking as if he was saying to himself, "You finally have met your match. Leave these people alone." That's what her husband looked like he was saying in his head.

The more we argued, the more intense the argument became, and I began to curse. My nephew grabbed me by the arm and led me back across the street. CJ got on the phone and called the police and played the victim. When the police arrived, they wanted to speak to both parties. I think they already knew CJ. Because the police were talking to my son and my nephew, they were very understanding of the situation that we were in, and the police talked with CJ and told her she can't be doing that—leaving letters and stuff on our cars. The police advised both parties to try to get along so they wouldn't have to come back out, that everyone is grown enough to try to be neighborly among one another. We all agreed and said okay.

So as time passed, we didn't have any more problems out of CJ. One day, I was in my garage, cleaning it out and sweeping. I had my music playing, and I turned around. CJ was standing behind me. When I say this lady had the opportunity to shoot me right there or do anything she wanted to do to me, she could have because I had no idea that someone was standing behind me, watching me that whole time.

That sneaky little heifer didn't say a word. Then when she saw that I almost had a heart attack, when I turned around and saw her standing there, she said, "I didn't mean to startle you. I'm sorry."

I said, "Yes, you scared me. I didn't have any idea that someone was behind me. But how can I help you?"

She said, "I just wanted to apologize to you for my behavior. I am so sorry, and I would very much like if you would accept my apology." And she went on to tell me the story about the people that lived there before us, how she turned them in because they were drug dealers and she had been watching them for months and she had all their transactions of drug activity on her camera, which was pointing at our house.

I was like to myself, *Man, you really take neighborhood watch to another level,* and I told her, "CJ, not all Black people are drug dealers. I'm sorry. We are not in that statistic, nor do we fit the scenario. We are hardworking people who are trying to make it in this world. My children have nine-to-five jobs. We are honest people."

She said again, "I'm sorry. I want us to be friends. I'm having a dinner tomorrow, and I want to invite you and let you know that you are welcome in the neighborhood. I wanted to bake you a cake, but my husband said you probably wouldn't accept it."

I said, "You're right. I probably wouldn't have accepted it because of the problems that we were having, but I do accept your apology, and I will try to make it to your party."

We talked a little while longer, and she left, and I knew damn well I wasn't going to her party; I still didn't trust her ass. I wanted to let her know you're looking at a boss. You're looking at a woman who owned her own business for twenty-three years, who had forty employees, who was the proud owner of ten vans that pick children up, who has a home larger than this one. I'm the proud owner of mobile homes and rent them out in the community, who bought her children three and a half acres of land that they can one day build their own house on. You are looking at a lady who has built a name in the community for being a successful entrepreneur. I wanted to let her know that you're not looking at a nobody; you're very much around Black royalty, baby. Don't judge a book by its cover, and definitely don't get it twisted. I might be going through hell now, but I have enjoyed these last twenty-three years of my life, baby; I have had mostly everything that I have wanted. I have driven and purchased some of the best cars on the market. I have visited places that I wanted to visit, so please don't let this Black face fool you.

After that, I didn't have any more trouble out of CJ. She would wave when she saw me, and I would always return that fake wave back. She was always cheerful, wanted to stop and talk when she would see me outside. You know that should have been the neighborly way when we first met. We weren't out to harm anyone. I think CJ realized that she met a Cindy, and it didn't feel good to get a dose of your own medicine. I think she came to the realization that maybe I was being an asshole. Maybe these people aren't so bad after all.

As the troubles were over with CJ, the trouble was not over at home with my family, with my children. Moving to Georgia almost destroyed my family. What was I thinking bringing them all the way up here in unfamiliar territory? My daughters had never lived outside Alabama, but I had just uprooted my entire family from everything that they knew and moved to a new state. But I was in too deep; I couldn't turn back now. I must stay at least a year and make this work. This was the best that I could do to try to keep my family together. It would be a difficult task. I did not realize how hard this had been for my kids. They were fighting their own battles, their own demons, and it will all play out. They thought they were ready because they were going to be with their mom, but I was no good for anyone in the condition that I was in. I wasn't healthy. I was mentally unstable. I wasn't the mother that they knew that they once had. I had become a stranger to myself.

I'm sure that they were wondering who I was. Also it would be days I didn't know if I was coming or going. Now, I'm in a new city, sleeping in a dark room again, crying and feeling miserable because now I realize that I have a criminal record that was following me. When I applied for jobs and the company did a background check on me, I wouldn't get the job—something I didn't think I would ever have to think about. It was so degrading to become the employee instead of the employer. All of this took me back to the day I had to go to court after my attorney made a plea deal with the DA for me and I received five years' probation and pay restitution for hard-earned money that I honestly made for an honest day's work. Those children never stayed out of day care unless they were sick or it was a holiday other than that they didn't miss a day. Like I said, I earned that money honestly.

"Do not take revenge, my dear friends, but leave room for God's wrath, for it is written: 'It is mine to avenge; I will repay,' says the Lord" (Rom. 12:19). I would listen to gospel music and pray. I have always been a praying person. I would always try to pray before leaving home in the mornings to go to work. I was damn near going crazy. I was getting on Facebook live sometimes. I would be drunk, and the times that I wasn't drunk, I don't even remember some of the things that I had said or done, but I'm pretty sure they were horrible. I think I was an embarrassment to my children. I'm sure they didn't like seeing me in that condition, but I was out of control, and no one could stop me—I couldn't stop myself. I couldn't balance out the different emotions and feelings, heartache, pain and suffering, and anxiety and depression. I was in such a dark space I didn't know if I was going to come out of it.

Vicki Yohe made a song called "I'm at Peace." It would soothe the soul. Marvin Sapp, Shirley Caesar, and many more gospel artists that I would listen to morning, midday, and at night—I have been worshipping with their music for years. I needed the substance. I needed to feel whole again. I needed to know that God still loves me. In one day, he would reward me for all my good deeds, and I will be at peace, but it still feels so unreachable. My children were suffering. I think it pushed my daughter to the edge because the day that she exploded on me, this was when I truly knew I was ready to go home to be with my God. I was in the car at the time with my daughter. I was taking her to work. She said she wouldn't be in this predicament if it wasn't for me, screaming and hollering at me. I could hardly drive her to work because my feeling was so hurt. To hear this coming from home now, it sounded like something her husband would say. Then she accused me of her losing everything in her life. I was devastated. I didn't know where to go or what to do. I wanted to jump from a cliff, drive away so no one could ever find me again because she had just confirmed everything that was being said about me—everything.

I was thinking about myself. How could I let my whole family get out in a new environment and expect them to survive? I couldn't help them anymore. What was I thinking? Bringing them here—what had I done? I was overwhelmed with guilt. My own child had lost respect and what seemed like a loss of love for me. The only person who has ever been there for me. I was driving, praying, and crying. I wanted to die right there at that very second. My children—they do hate me. I am a disappointment to them. I did let them down, and here I am, a nobody. All the rumors are true. I shouldn't have been in business. I have ruined so many lives, and my character will forever be destroyed. I had no one to turn to for support.

I drove all the way from Suwanee, Georgia, down to Union City, Georgia. It's an hour drive, and I sat in the back of Pizza Hut parking lot debating about how I was going to kill myself, and I thought I had nothing else to live for. Of course, I loved my grandkids. They were innocent. They knew nothing about what happened. They didn't know that their grandmother was in all this trouble. They didn't know that her life had made a turn for the worse.

I was thinking, *Should I try to stay here for them?* But then again, I said, "No. They have parents. They'll be okay. I've raised my kids. They will be okay too. They have time to rebuild their lives, so whatever they think about me now is on them because I did the best that I could do. I brought them from an abusive marriage that I was in, and I built a home. I tried to give them everything that I never had—all their heart desires. So if they're not proud of that, I'm sorry. There's nothing else I can do," as I was sitting there with tears all over my face. I didn't have enough tissue to wipe the tears from my eyes.

I thought about one person that I could always call, and she would always give me good, sound, firm advice. That was my niece Toya. She's my niece by marriage and my best friend. Then I called her, and we talked for hours. I assured her that I wouldn't harm myself. Everyone was blowing up my phone, and I wouldn't answer—even the daughter that just told me that I had ruined her life.

How could she say that? I had given them everything that they had. I didn't complain when I bought them their multiple cars and purchased them their first mobile home and not to mention all the years of getting what they all wanted. What made me go home was when my daughter texted me and said if I didn't come home, she was going to make matters worse, and I knew what that meant. So I drove home, but my mind was already made up: I couldn't continue to live in this cruel world. I hated disappointing my children and knowing that they think so less of me. My husband had left me, and all the people that said they cared—they weren't here for me. Employees that I used to talk to on the phone sometimes just because we had a close relationship, evidently, we weren't as close as I thought because my phone stopped ringing. What was my purpose or my reason to continue to live? I needed God to show me a sign because if not, the flesh had weakened to my lowest point. I had never wanted to give up on anything before in my life—certainly not life itself. I used to think how a person can give up on life and commit suicide. I'm not questioning that statement anymore because now I understand just how close you can come to ending it all.

So when I went to bed that night, I asked God to forgive me for what I was about to do. I lay in my bed. I got two different types of sleeping pills that I take, and I started to take one after the other, talking to God and taking my pills and telling myself, "Hi, I am a failure. Oh, how I have failed life and how I failed my family."

The situation that I was in had defeated me. Every time I would feel myself getting ready to fall asleep, I would take some more pills, and I was talking to myself about how I was not loved nor appreciated. I was talking and laughing, crying, telling God, "I'm ready." I was pitiful. I was just saying, "Lord, why? What did I do to deserve this, Lord? Lord, why did this have to happen to me?"

I was just crying and taking pills. I kept saying, "They don't want me around anymore."

When I wrote my children's father a goodbye letter, I knew I had lost sense of reality. When I reached out to my abuser, I didn't know if I was seeking gratification of knowing that all he had said about me all those years ago was true. Reaching out to him during a suicidal mission somehow gave me some crazy sense of satisfaction in knowing at the end, "You were right all along. You said I didn't come from anything. You said I would never be anything. You said that no man wanted me. You said I didn't come from shit and would never have shit. I accomplish everything that you said. How could I have been so stupid thinking that I was somebody, that I had made it, and that I had become this successful person in life?"

My God just took it all away—or should I say people took it all away because I really don't want to blame God for this because God doesn't hurt his children; he loves us. I wanted to go to this place where God said there is no more crying, no more suffering; we won't have any more trials and tribulations to go through. We won't have people being jealous, no more backstabbing. I wanted to go to that place. I still believe in God. I still had faith in God. I still trust him. It was the flesh that was so weak. The flesh had taken over. I don't know how I was able to even function.

It's funny how God has a plan to save you. When it is not your time, you are not going anywhere. How did I call the hospital that night? I called them and asked them for some depression pills, and

I spoke to them about suicide. I know that the lady kept me on the phone a long time, asking me questions about suicide. I was trying to get some more pills. I still don't know how many pills I actually had taken, but this lady won't leave me alone, asking me all sorts of questions and telling me to come in to see them so they could help me.

I said, "I don't want your help. I need my medicine."

After she couldn't get me to say that I wouldn't commit suicide, instead, she started using psychology on me. At the time, I didn't know that was what she was doing, but once this all played out, I figured it out. She told me, "If you come to the clinic, we will give you your medicine," and that was all I wanted to hear—that she was going to give me some medicine. After I got off the phone with her, I didn't know if I was living or dead.

I just remembered my son was shaking me and screaming out, "Mama, Mama, wake up, wake up!" I remembered him saying, "Oh my god, oh my god, Mama, Mama, wake up, wake up."

I opened my eyes, and he said, "Mama, I thought you was dead. Why are all these pills in your bed?"

I said, "I was trying to commit suicide, but it didn't work, but I need for you to take me to the hospital to get my medicine. Can you take me there?"

He said, "Yeah, Mama, I'll take you to get your medicine."

As we walked down the stairs to get ready to go get in the car, my nephew was coming up the stairs. He was looking at me strange.

He said, "Auntie, your eyes are red as fire," and all I was thinking to myself, *Thank God that I didn't succeed*, but when we arrived at the hospital, all I could remember was the lady used Psychology 101 on me that night. God wasn't ready for me. Somehow, someway, I survived through all those pills that I had taken. So when I went in the hospital, I didn't know what I had in store for me. They asked me my name, and they told me they had been waiting for me. The lady asked me if I had my purse with me and she needed my ID.

After she got my ID, she told my son, "You can wait outside in the waiting area. She is in good hands now."

I still didn't realize what was happening. We went through a door, and it locked behind us. I was following her because all I wanted were my pills, but as I walked through another door, I could hear that door lock behind me as well. It took the lady a long time to return to the room. As I was waiting on her, I tried to open the door so I could leave, but the door wouldn't open. I started banging on the door and hollering for someone to come unlock this door and let me out, and then here came the lady with some keys in her hand.

I said, "My son is waiting for me. We've got to go, and why are these doors locked?" I couldn't open the door.

She said, "Your son has left. You have been admitted to the mental institution. You tried to commit suicide."

I looked at her, and I said, "I called y'all so I could get my medication. You cannot keep me here against my will. I want to call my son so he can come pick me up."

She said, "No, ma'am, anytime someone calls into this facility and admit to wanting to harm their self, we are allowed to hold you for a mental evaluation."

I said, "I didn't call y'all."

She said, "Yes, you did," and then she started to tell me some of the things I talked to the counselor that handled my phone call that night.

I said to myself, *These people recorded me.* I knew there was no way I was going to get out of that facility.

After what she told me, I was like, *Damn, I thought I called a hospital. I called a freaking mental institution. Girl, how are you going to get out of here? You did it this time. You fucked up big time. All those damn pills—that's what's got you here.*

I was still high as a kite. I felt defeated, so when I realized I wasn't getting out of there, I went to the room they gave me, and I lay down and went to sleep. The next morning after I sobered up, I couldn't think of anything but how I was going to get out of this place because they were talking about keeping me a long time. I had been assigned counselors and doctors.

I said, "These people think I'm crazy. I've got to get out of here." I could only get a couple of phone calls out to my family, and it was certain times, and the food was nasty. I said to myself, "This is some bullshit, girl, you really done it this time." They wanted my doctor's name to get a list of all my medications.

They told me, "You don't have to worry about medicine in here. You're going to get all the medicine you want."

I said to myself, *You trying to be funny?* Ain't shit funny to me, but at the same time, being in that facility—it's crazy, but I felt at peace. I felt relieved. I felt for one time in my life that I didn't have to worry about making anybody happy. I didn't have to worry about what's going on outside in the world. I didn't have to worry about anyone depending on me. I felt free. After all that drama that I had endured, I felt free, but I was still trying to figure out a way to get out of this facility.

When it was time for my phone call, I called my son Trevon, and I told him to "Get in touch with Bobby, let him know where I'm at and for him to come and try to get me out of this place."

I promise you God works in mysterious ways, and he works everything out in your favor. I'm having to have sessions with my counselor, and the doctors come around to see me and to talk about "How are you feeling?" and what I was going through. "Do you still have suicidal thoughts?"

I had a morning doctor, and I had an evening doctor—two different doctors. All of this is a bunch of crap. On my second day of being in the facility, this was the second time that they had given me my meds given by a med tech. Let me tell you how God works: so it's two patients in a room. Here came the med tech. He gave me my medication. He looked at my bracelet, asked me if this is my name and date of birth, and I said yes.

As he proceeded to give me my medication and he put them in my hand one by one, when he got to the red pill, I told him, "That's not my medicine."

He told me, "These are your pills," and I said, "I know what type of medicine I take. This is not my medicine."

He said, "Yes, this is your medicine," and he insisted that I take the medication, and he was so demanding. I don't know why I didn't refuse, but I didn't want to take them, and he went on to say, "I have a list of all your medication," and he suggested that I take them. He watched to see if I swallowed the pills then. After taking this medication, I can say not even a good thirty minutes later, I started to feel sick at the stomach. Then I started throwing up. I went to sit in the dayroom to watch television, thinking that I would feel better. I was feeling so sick, and another resident noticed, and she went to get the nurse. The nurse asked me if I was okay, and I said, "No, I don't feel good." I told the nurse that I had told the med tech that he was giving me the wrong medication, that the medicine wasn't my medicine, but he insisted that I take it, and I took it, and ever since I took the medicine, I had been sick, and I kept throwing up. I wanted to go to my room, but I didn't think I could get up. I was so weak that I couldn't even get up out of the chair.

The nurse told me that she would be back to check on me, and I told her that I would sit out in the dayroom for just a little while. The workers behind the glass—they're looking out at us in the dayroom, and I was thinking that they noticed that there's something wrong with me. One of the other workers came and asked me if I was okay, and I told her no.

I said again, "I kept telling that guy that that wasn't my medicine, but he made me take it, and I've been sick ever since I took the medicine, and I feel like I'm going to pass out."

She said, "Can you stand up so I can help you go to your room to lie down?"

I said, "Yes, but I don't think I can get up." I was so weak.

She said, "Wait right here. Let me go get a wheelchair."

She went and got a wheelchair, and two people had to pick me up and put me in the wheelchair. They rolled me to my room, and they put me in the bed, and I stayed in that bed all day. The workers at the facility kept checking on me because they knew that the guy had made a mistake and gave me the wrong medication. I could see the overwhelming concern; it was written all over their faces. They were worried about me, and they were hoping that nothing happened to me. I don't think they had a patient that had been that sick where she couldn't even walk after taking medicine. I believed this guy gave me the lady's medication that was in the room with me.

I knew I had them at this point, that they were going to have to let me out of this place. I wasn't really worried about that at the time; I was just hoping that I was going to be okay. I believe they knew that a lawsuit would probably be filed against them if anything happens to me. So I used it to my advantage. When I spoke to my son Trevon, I told him the entire episode that happened to me in the facility and for him to call Bobby to get me out of this facility. After my son spoke to Bobby, he came straight to Atlanta to the facility where I was. One of the counselors came to my room and said, "It's not a visiting day for relatives, but your husband is here to see you, so let's get you out of bed and take you to the dayroom so you can have your visit."

This is what you call covering that ass. She had to help me get in the wheelchair and roll me up front. They let him come back to see me, and he said, "So they gave you the wrong medicine."

"Yes, they are supposed to be saving me, but they damn near killed me." I told Bobby, "This is how I can get out of this facility." We were whispering because we didn't want anyone to hear our plan. "You've got to go and tell them they have to release me because they have given me the wrong medication, plus I've got to be in Alabama for court in three days."

He said, "You're right."

After we talked for a while, Bobby said, "I'm going to speak to one of the nurses, and I'm going to get you out of here."

I was so glad to hear that, but I didn't know if it was going to work or not, so I waited to see what was going to happen. When Bobby got through talking to those people and advising them of the potential lawsuit that they almost killed me in there with the medication that they gave me and informing them that I had to go to court in Alabama, if not, I could go to jail for ten years, Bobby said he had never fought that hard for me. I think he was proud of himself, but before they released me, I had to talk to both doctors and the counselor before I could leave. They wanted to know what all had happened to me in Alabama, and they wanted to know why I wanted to commit suicide. I told the doctor about how my business failed and how I got in trouble; I told him about my failed marriage, that we are trying to work things out, and I told him that I was having problems when it came to my children, but that could easily be resolved. I told the doctor about the jail time I was facing if I did not appear in court.

He did show some sympathy. He also said, "At this point, we are responsible for you," and he said, "If I release you, you have to assure me that you will not harm yourself in any kind of way," and I convinced those doctors I'm not going to do anything to myself, that I really need to get back home and handle this situation because I want to go back home to my family and I made a mistake and that I would not do it again.

After both doctors consulted with each other, one of them came back to my room and told me he would release me to my husband. I was ecstatic, and I was also proud of Bobby for standing up for me this one time since we've been together. It took all day for Bobby to get me released from that facility, but when we left there, Bobby told me, "Those people had no intention of letting you out." The only thing that saved me was the fact that one of their employees had given me the wrong medicine and how sick I was from it.

When I tell you God is a miracle worker, that's exactly who he is—a miracle worker. God made sure that those people were going to let me out of their facility so I could be able to go back home. I made it to court in Alabama. After court, I returned home to Georgia, very much relieved to be out of the facility, but still I was completely broken, and I continued to cry and pray, asking God for answers. I just did not understand why my life was in such turmoil. What have I done to deserve all this misfortune? God, haven't I been a good server? Haven't I done for others like you told us to do? Haven't I been good to thy neighbor? Haven't I done, Lord, everything that you wanted me to do? Were you not pleased with the things that I've done? I thought I had passed the test. My heart is pure, and I am sincere. Yet I didn't understand—why would you forsake me?

I walked around with no money and just wondered when I would get my breakthrough that God promised me was coming. My children walked around not talking to each other. I looked like I had aged from all the worrying. My sister Carolyn who was accused of the same crime, she would call and check on me. After twenty years of not being a family, we hashed out our differences because we both had lost everything that we had worked for. The arguments didn't matter anymore. We could talk and talk about how broken our lives are. It was like getting to know someone for the first time all over again. Now it makes sense—all I ever wanted was my big sister back, and she couldn't see that. She didn't understand that I felt like she raised me, she taught me a lot of stuff that I didn't know, and she would listen to me about my problems with my boyfriends and husbands. She really made a great impact in my life, and when I lost her by me being so stubborn, it really didn't matter, but there have been times that I did reach out to her, and she rejected me. I'm not the type to hang around when I'm not wanted, and I know when I'm not wanted around. So it was easy for me to just let it all go. I had learned to live alone, not being a part of the family that didn't bother me. Yes, sometimes it hurt. Sometimes I would cry, but the hardcore side of me wouldn't let me keep going back, saying I'm sorry for something I didn't know I was even sorry about. Family can sometimes be your worst enemies. We are supposed to be the ones that love each other when no one else loves us, and we wonder how our business get in the street.

Most of the time it is a family member that tells your business, and it's a family member who's not rooting for you to make it. I've had several of those kinds of family members. I learned to live with it, and I learned to live without them. Carolyn and I had conversations about how we were going to get our feet back on the ground. She was trying to re-open her day care.

I didn't even want to hear the word *day care*. I was on a different path, believing in what God had told me that this was my time to be happy, this was my time to shine, this was my time to travel to go places I'd had never dreamed I would go, this was my time to have wealth and keep it, and this was my time to reclaim my good name I will receive from all the good deeds that he had allowed me to give to others. This was my time to tell people my story and what God has taken from me and what he is about to restore to me. Every man and woman has a battle to fight, and only the strong will survive. Your battle is not my battle; your fight is not my fight. We all have our own demons, trials, and tribulations to conquer only by the grace of God, and the few and faithful will defeat this battle. Keep believing and trusting in him. Build the flesh so you can withstand the spiritual battles ahead that has been placed in our lives. So many people have told me simply, "You are one of God's warriors, and he gives his toughest battles to his strongest soldiers." As I struggled with that statement for a long time, I was truly in a battle of good and evil, and I meant that I was going to continue to fight for God. I continued praying and worshipping and believing that God didn't lead me in my life with the interchange of failure, but he wants all his children to succeed. God said, "You will be inspired, and you will see your purpose."

I mustered up the courage to apply for jobs online to go to the temporary agencies and apply for jobs despite my background. Oh, I was worshipping and praising God and being joyful in my praise as I listen to my songs, and I danced to the music and was just loving on God, believing in God just like I used to. Despite all I've been through, I started to feel better about myself. I went out and got a job, and I started writing my book. So now I finally realized my story—my life—can inspire someone else who is suicidal, suffering from depression, someone else who has lost it all. I wanted to start a foundation to help other people like me who had been accused of committing a crime. Did they really? For someone who has been humiliated, I want people to realize that your life doesn't stop when these labels are placed on you.

The legal system is designed to ruin your life. First, your application is put in the trash because they wouldn't dare let a felon work in their facility or plant or store, not even a service station or grocery store. Then people look at you funny when they know you have a felony because they judge you because the justice system says you are a bad person even though you have proven in your community that you are a respectable person with morals and that you have a great character. You have built that throughout the years—that doesn't matter anymore. They just throw you out like trash and to the wolves and say, "Survive anyway you can. There isn't anyone who is going to help you."

You must go into survival mode and figure out how you're going to make it because once you were a business owner and you lose it, you know your brain is stuck on being an entrepreneur and you're trying to figure out how you are going to get your hands on some money to start this business. People are not willing to give you a second chance; that's why I got to be the person that I have always been—out to help others—but this time I'm included in that bunch. I'm a felon now until I can get these charges expunged off my record. This is what I must live with, but it doesn't have to stop my life. I want to build low-income homes for people who have been incarcerated, who have nowhere to live and their family doesn't want them to come back home; for people who are just like me, had their own business and they lost it all, and now they don't have any money, and they just need some money in their hands to help them get back in the community.

God put me on a mission, and this is my purpose: God wants me to use my voice, intellect and Testimony to help someone else. I want to be able to create jobs so people can rebuild their lives. I mean, what is a person to do who have these labels on them? Some people are not deserving of the labels that we have been given. I want to do something about that. I have always enjoyed helping other people. This time, I get to help myself as well as others. Luckily, I didn't go to prison, but I'm a prisoner in my home because no one wants to be bothered with a felon. No one trusts a felon. No one will help you raise money, and no one will donate to you. It's a shame how society turns their back on fellow citizens, and I'm not just saying it because now I'm one.

I'm saying it because I never realized what these people were going through before I got this label. Now I really, really realize what they go through in this world. You are an outcast; you are not wanted. I wonder what would have happened to the people that I served in my community for twenty-three years—what would have happened to all those people if I would have turned my back on them? If my fist was closed? If I didn't believe in giving and just receiving? Who came to me looking for help when they couldn't get it anywhere else? Where would their children be now if I wouldn't have been there for them when they couldn't put food on the table or pay their light bill? Things that I've done to help them out when they were at their lowest point in their life?

But none of those people came to my rescue at my time of need, but I'm okay with that because I don't look to man for my blessings; I look to God for all my blessings. I get on my knees, and I tell God what I want and what I need. But in this world, sometimes we do have to call upon one another to lend a helping hand. You will never know who you might need one day, and we cannot live in this world alone. So with that being said, I didn't let what happen to me destroy my world. After being in a mental institution because I attempted suicide, I thought I didn't want to live. I decided to live my life and began to take back my life and start sounding like the old Cynthia again. I started to love myself again, and I was even considering having a relationship with my husband that left, but some things are better left alone. We get along better living separately. I respected him for standing in the gap for me this time when I needed him the most.

It had been a year since I had been to church. I met a lady on a job assignment I was on. We became friends almost instantly. She had a calm spirit about herself. We were talking on the phone one night, and I asked her where she attended church, and she told me she sent the address through a text message. The very next day, which was Sunday, I went to her church. As I was sitting there, it wasn't the traditional Black church that I was used to. As the service went on, I noticed people are going to the altar and the pastor prayed for them and touched them. They were falling out.

I said to myself, "This is one of those sanctified churches that my momma always told me not to go to."

As I was sitting there, listening to the message—it was the month of February, to be exact—as the pastor continued with his message, he was saying stuff like, "Whatever you are asking God for, he told me to tell you this is your time. This is your season. If you want to open that business, this is the time. If you are writing a book, he said finish it now because this is your season."

I started looking around the church because I know I have been procrastinating on writing my book. I said, "I hear you, Lord." I knew God was talking to me. I was meant to be there at that church that day. I truly believe God sends messages in all kinds of ways. My eyes and ears are glued to the words coming out of this pastor's mouth. I want some of that healing he is placing upon them; I knew the Holy Spirit was there because I could feel it. I wasn't going to abandon God, because he loves me, and he hasn't left me, and he saved my life.

When you go to church, you feel the message is always about you, and this message truly was for me. As I went to get up from my seat, Bobby grabbed my hand and said, "I know you are not going up there."

I said, "Yes, I am," as I walked to the altar. I didn't care who was there; God was calling me up there so I could get this touch of him through this pastor because my soul was yearning for that anointing touch from God. I needed to be delivered through Jesus Christ my Savior.

When the pastor whispered in my ear and spoke the words from God, he touched my forehead, and I could feel the Holy Spirit, and for the first time in my life, I truly felt the Holy Spirit touch me, and I passed out. When I woke up, I was lightheaded and stumbled back to my seat. I felt refreshed. I wanted to hear every word that God was speaking to me through this man. I truly knew God wasn't finished with me, and he is going to allow me to accomplish all my dreams. When I and my family moved back to Alabama in August 2020, my family had mended itself. My children had gotten back close to one another. We made a family group chat. Everyone treats everyone like we are family. We talk on the phone almost daily. I am so thankful and grateful to God that he saved my life and then he allowed me to live again and to be here for my children and my grandchildren because all that I ever truly wanted was to be a beacon for my family.

I truly believe in God's Word. He said vengeance was his and to let him deal with the heathens. My sister Carolyn Starr Wilkerson passed away from COVID-19 on August 12, 2020. May she rest in peace. She didn't get a chance to witness the Lee County district attorney that indicted us become a victim of his own deceptions. DA Brandon Hughes was charged with seven counts of fraud and using his office for personal gain and ethical violations. I'd say the pot is not calling the kettle black. He said, "If you come to Lee County and commit a crime, you will be punished." He didn't realize he was being watched by his own. Thank you, Lee County, for dealing with your own hypocrites. There are some crooked people in high places hiding behind their positions and the authority that they have been given. So all of us who were victims of Brandon Hughes, we are calling for all his cases to be reviewed. The governor of Alabama and the attorney general's office are not doing their jobs for the citizens of Lee County if our cases are not reviewed. So let's be honest if you are receiving government assistance and you are not being honest about your situation. Whether it's financial or whether it's your personal status and you are not telling the complete truth, you are committing fraud. We all are guilty of that, so don't be so quick to judge someone else 'cause you are only a step away from your felony. Stop judging people and look in the mirror. You will be surprised at who you see.

Thank you, Lord. You have allowed me to escape the hands of the devourer. Truly God has been good to me. I feel stress-free. I am happy to be in my home in Alabama. My life would never be the same again, and I have accepted that, but that doesn't mean that I won't succeed in different areas in my life.

My children are back in their homes. I wouldn't trade my grandkids for anything in the world. Now my middle daughter has a daughter and two sons, and my oldest daughter has a son and a daughter. And my son? Well, he's good. It doesn't matter what we went through. It happened for a reason, and we went through it together. I'm still trying to save the home that we built for our family, the home that I love and worked so hard to maintain. These experiences have made us better people.

One thing about life is that you never know when it's going to throw you a curveball. Toya has the dance team again with a new group of children, and my granddaughter Jer'meria is dancing her little heart away. I have strengthened my belief in God and re-dedicated my life to Christ. He is a God of impossibility; there's not one miracle that he can't perform. Your life is in his hands, so allow him to guide you and walk with you.

When the walls in your life begin to fall, your foundation begins to crack, and everything inside feels like it's falling apart, just look to God. He is waiting with open arms. And he's watching every step you take. If you let him lead your path, you won't lose your direction. In life, always listen to that little voice; and when you get on that wrong path, don't let go of God because he said in his Word, I will never leave you nor forsake you. —Deuteronomy 31:8

He will always lead you back in the right direction if you let him. He is a God of signs and wonders, with miraculous power. When that little voice whispers in your ear, listen carefully. He's speaking to you.

Destruction does not come without a warning. Keep praying, trusting, and believing in God. Walk by faith and not by sight; seeing will deceive you, but faith will never fail you. Rather than dwell on the past, he is committed to the future. I have truly been given a second chance at life, and I'm taking it all the way back to the top. Success, blessing, and God's favor is my *name*: Cynthia LaJune Jones.

I can do all things through Christ
which strengtheneth me.
—Philippians 4:13

ABOUT THE AUTHOR

As a little girl, Cynthia had dreams of becoming someone bigger than life, not settling for what life was throwing at her, always aspiring to become the person that she dreamed of becoming. She is ambitious, loyal, kind, compassionate, loving; and Cynthia became a successful land, home, and business owner.

Being a survivor of domestic violence gave her the strength to grab a hold of her dream and make it become reality because the abuse made her realize if she can survive that, she can accomplish anything.

These last couple of years have changed her life in a way that she never imagined. She has had time to sit back and evaluate her whole existence and say "God," not "Why?" but so many reasons.

Printed in the USA
CPSIA information can be obtained
at www.ICGtesting.com
LVHW062329190124
769097LV00019B/368